INNOVATION
FROM
WITHIN

A leader's guide to driving rapid
digital transformation

TJEERD HUNNEKENS

T0333632

R^ethink

First published in Great Britain in 2024
by Rethink Press (www.rethinkpress.com)

© Copyright Tjeerd Hunnekens

This book is dedicated to the ones who stood by me in every step I made, from the beginning till the end.

To my partner, Madiha; thank you for your continuous support and encouragement. Your belief in me gave me the strength to see this project through.

To my beloved children, Casper, Xander, and Suze; and Madiha's daughter, Sarah. Thanks for your presence in my life, which is a constant reminder of the importance of family. Your love and understanding made the journey of writing this book more meaningful.

To my mother, who has been a beacon of light and a source of love and support throughout my life; thank you for being my rock. You have been my constant inspiration, and I am forever grateful for your being.

Contents

Foreword

What is the essence of success? Have you ever paused to consider the architects of transformation, those who forge the path from the mundane to the extraordinary? What is it that sets them apart—their strategies, their charisma, or their steadfast determination? In a world where complexity reigns and change is the only constant, how can we as change leaders navigate with impact? I found this book unravels the very essence of digital transformation and describes a valuable path in how to be successful.

From my own experience, I can say that in a world where the journey from inception to achievement is often fraught with complexity, the importance of a pragmatic approach cannot be overstated. This book stands full of pragmatism, where each insight is not just a theory, but could be a blueprint for action.

And now, allow me to introduce myself—a fellow traveler on the road of change, empowerment, and technological evolution. For decades, I have ventured through the corridors of the technology, a voyage that saw me not just as a participant, but a driver of progress. I've been described as a change enabler, seamlessly merging the realms of technology and transformation. My passion lies in crafting organizations that thrive daily, and in nurturing teams to lead.

This book is the brainchild of Tjeerd—a name synonymous with experience, results, and a profound understanding of the human element. With large number of years under his belt, his journey is not just a chronicle but a symphony of insights curated from the classroom of real-world encounters. Each chapter is a testament to his intuition, his resilience, and his ability to turn obstacles into steppingstones. Embedded within these pages are the very threads that connect success and failure—real-world examples, lessons learned through sweat and trial. Every capture resonates with the pulse of practicality, the very heartbeat of successful execution.

Tjeerd's approach in this book is both unique and relatable. An exquisite blend of "the good, the bad, and the ugly", all underscored by a resolute positivity. His narrative style is embracing challenges, in celebrating setbacks as catalysts for growth. This approach makes this book a companion. In weaving his narrative, Tjeerd takes the familiar of established models such as Scenario thinking, Mindset of action, Start with Why and What, Innovation culture … and crafts a tapestry. He has the ability to take the tried and true—those well-known models and frameworks—and meld them into something relevant and actionable solutions.

In closing, it is with great enthusiasm that I recommend this book to all change leaders across industries. Tjeerd's narrative is a symphony of experience and positivity that has the potential to guide your own journey of transformation. Embrace its lessons, revel in its insights, and allow it to be the compass that propels you toward successful digital transformation.

Enjoy your read!

Amir Arooni
Executive Vice President and CIO at
Discover Financial Services, USA

Introduction

Dear CIOs, IT directors, change leaders, department heads, and IT-orientated leaders,

Imagine this: you're in the middle of a digital transformation, but it's not going well. Perhaps your plans to innovate have left you spinning your wheels in the mud. Your company is not taking full advantage of the latest technologies and approaches and is therefore struggling to compete. It's your job to come up with a solution—but how?

You wouldn't have reached your level at work if you weren't highly competent, but you need a little help.

Perhaps your organization is implementing a combined methodology such as Agile DevOps to improve collaboration, but many departments are still siloed and resistant to change. Maybe there is a culture creep in the organization, where traditional hierarchical structures are being replaced by a more collaborative and decentralized approach, but not everyone is adapting well to this change.

It could be that your digital strategy seems to live only in the boardroom, with little input or involvement from the rest of the company. Despite your company having a wealth of talented employees, it is not effectively using their skills and talents to drive innovation. It's as if innovation is viewed as something separate from the rest of the company rather than it being integrated into everyday operations. This is similar, for example, to a company's finance department having a separate boardroom-only status, which also causes friction and limits collaboration across departments.

For your business—or your department—to stay competitive, you have to make the digital transformation work. Otherwise, you will not be effectively engaging with customers or addressing their needs.

If you feel overwhelmed, you are not alone. I see businesses everywhere struggling to translate strategy into successful innovative implementations, no matter how straightforward they might seem. At board and execution levels, people are suffering and losing motivation. In some cases, employees can even end up needing time off work due to stress caused by organizational defects, often exacerbated by the fast pace of technological innovation.

From over thirty years of diverse experience and practical insights in innovation, platform development, advanced digitization, operation, and leadership—including numerous digital transformations for large corporations—I have gathered the expertise to help you overcome common challenges like scaling, talent utilization, change portfolio management, and mindset enhancement.

Over the past twenty years, I have executed many groundbreaking strategy implementations within leading financial institutions. These include:

- Merging the IT of two banks

- Advising board members how to get their party master data management system into a good execution state

- Driving the IT transformational program for ING in the Netherlands to pave the way for global rollout

- Establishing a part of the ING platform foundation to run one IT solution in many countries

I have also been responsible for several operational units; and in my role as a manager, I am often involved as a lead in crisis situations.

In leading change experts, project and program managers, and integrators, I have acquired the skills and knowledge to successfully manage complex transformation projects. I have led teams through model shifts from Waterfall to Agile Scrum methodology—a journey we will touch on in more detail in this book—enabling those teams to work more efficiently and effectively while delivering high-quality results.

Introducing a worldwide IT foundational platform based on a micro services architecture has given me a deep understanding of how to navigate the complexities of large-scale digital projects. (One could compare this platform with the App store functionality of iOS.) I understand the importance of effective communication, stakeholder engagement, and change management, in ensuring successful implementation and adoption of technological programs.

My experience as a global (transformation) lead has given me valuable insights into how cultural differences can affect project delivery and the overall success of digital transformation initiatives. I am also a holistic life coach, with a focus on business coaching. My central question is, What do you want to get out of your life?, with the aim of any individual's work environment changing to reflect their personal goals and values.

Overall, my diverse experiences and practical insights make me an ideal partner for you in the successful navigation of the challenges of digital transformation and in achieving your business goals. In *Innovation From Within*, I have compiled personal experiences, along with relevant insights from other experts, to reinforce my views and help you effectively prepare for the digital era.

Today's dynamic business landscape is dominated by generative artificial intelligence (AI) and pioneering companies, which are gradually substituting human labor with AI. The wheels of evolution are turning, reshaping our understanding of business. This transformative journey will not only redefine the way we operate but also prompt us to adopt new modes of thinking.

As AI edges us closer to a digitized realm, where the boundaries between the physical and virtual worlds blur, it is possible to envision a future where you can inspect a plant on one side of the globe in the morning, engage in a vibrant international event in the afternoon, and unwind with friends in your hometown in the evening, all while being virtually present through your digital twin. The convergence of hologram technology and the forthcoming Wi-Fi 6, Wi-Fi 7, and beyond promises to bring this within reach.

Does this imply that machines will seize control? Absolutely not. Your role as a chief information officer or other digital leader is crucial; you cannot afford to engage in idle attempts at steering your business in a new direction. This is precisely where I aim to lend my support through my RAPID Digital Transformation Model—a blueprint tailored specifically for you, laid out in Part Two of this book, to take you through the transformation journey:

1. **R: Research your market**

   - exploring your situation to determine your (IT) strategy

2. **A: Actualize your digital strategy**

   - building a successful executable digital strategy; making it real

3. **P: Plan for success**

   - anticipating hurdles with a realistic plan

4. **I: Innovate through transformation**

   - transforming your business into the new paradigm of digital

5. **D: Drive growth**

   - running your business in a digital environment

The RAPID Digital Transformation Model focuses on the 20% foundation you need to have in place to get your organization into an innovative state, from which 80% of work can be successfully completed. I will offer practical insights and strategies that will help you prepare for the digital era, overcome common challenges, and succeed in your digital transformation journey. You can also use the model effectively for a department or nonprofit organization transformation, focusing on each phase as if the department or nonprofit organization were a company.

Whether you're starting out on your journey or looking to course-correct a stalled initiative, this model will help. By adopting the RAPID Digital Transformation Model, and reflecting on the examples that illustrate each phase, you will be better equipped to navigate the digital transformation landscape.

Innovation From Within will inspire you to unleash your potential smoothly and efficiently and that of your organization as you take your place in the digital era. The book will show you how to:

- Adopt a strategic approach and leverage your existing resources to achieve your goals

- Discover measures that can be put in place to prevent, detect, and respond to incidents

- Realize the benefits of replacing legacy systems with modern, cloud-based solutions

- Learn how to introduce a robust monitoring system that allows you to go forward with confidence

- Glimpse new possibilities for citizen development as an empowering, transformative force within organizations, which delivers on speed and cost-efficiency

- Uncover the potential for sustainable growth and connection offered by the metaverse

Overall, you will gain a deeper understanding of the challenges and opportunities associated with digital transformation, and learn how to develop a strategic plan to address them.

Through examples drawn from my personal experience, we will follow the challenges that organizations face in keeping pace with the ever-evolving digital landscape. By applying the principles outlined in this book, you too can successfully navigate the challenges and achieve success.

Innovation is not something that can be imposed from the outside—it must come from within our organizations. It is only by cultivating a mindset of creativity, curiosity, and collaboration that we can truly unlock our full potential and drive meaningful change.

PART ONE
GET READY TO DRIVE DIGITAL CHANGE

Ideas are like seeds: only a few reach fertile
ground and prosper into fullness.

1
The New Digital Transformation Leaders

In this chapter I will show the latest trends in organizational leadership and explore the importance of cultivating the right mindset to promote innovation and growth from within. It's a journey of self-discovery and self-improvement.

Before you embark on the journey, take a moment to ponder the title of this book, *Innovation From Within*. It hints at a powerful truth: True innovation and growth must come from within an organization's leadership. This principle holds true not only in the business world but also in our personal lives. Just as we must take full responsibility for our own happiness and fulfillment, organizational leaders must take full responsibility for the success and innovation of their companies. As a leader, it is your responsibility to take charge of everything that happens within your organization, regardless of the outcome. One could argue that the actions of a predecessor may have played a role in certain circumstances, but even that shows how a proactive leader should have been able to anticipate and mitigate negative consequences.

In my journey of becoming a change leader, I had to start by believing in the power of transformation. I was drawn to the idea of creating positive change and making a real impact. At first I was purely goal-orientated, driven by the desire to achieve specific outcomes. This led me to delve into the world of change management, where I eagerly absorbed knowledge and faced numerous challenges, which eventually became stepping stones of wisdom. Along the way, I learned not only about change but also about understanding myself and connecting with others on a personal level.

Taking on the role of a change leader required me to be adaptable and embrace new strategies, even if some seemed risky. I soon realized that it wasn't just about reaching the goals I had set out to achieve; it was equally about the journey itself and the meaningful impact I could make along the way. I firmly held on to the value of integrity, consistently choosing the ethical path, even when this posed difficulties. Collaboration and respecting diverse viewpoints emerged as crucial facets of my leadership philosophy.

As time went on, I naturally assumed the position of a guide, helping my team members grow and celebrating each achievement, no matter how small. These celebrations fostered a sense of unity and accomplishment among us. Reflecting on my journey, I see a trail marked by hard work, learning from setbacks, and empowering others. My evolution—from an individual with a passion for transformation to a change leader—has been a personal transformation. This ongoing journey continues to shape my approach, reminding me that the path itself holds immense value, and that by embracing both the journey and the goals, meaningful change becomes the compass that guides my fellow team members into the future.

Having shared my personal journey, I invite you now to examine with me the trends, behavior mindsets, and key characteristics of successful digital leaders. Furthermore, I will underline the importance of visualization, which begins with you as a leader.

The top trends for 2024

Firstly, it's valuable to embrace a curiosity for innovation regardless of your background. Think about how different elements can come together to solve problems, even if they're outside your usual domain.

In the technology landscape, there are several note-worthy developments for 2024 that you should keep an eye on:[1]

1. **AI and machine learning:** These technologies power various applications such as chatbots, voice assistants, and predictive analytics. They are poised to find even more applications in the near future.

2. **Cloud computing:** This enables businesses to remotely store and access data, providing flexibility to scale infrastructure as needed.

3. **The internet of Things (IoT):** The IoT connects everyday devices to the internet, allowing remote monitoring and control.

4. **Cybersecurity:** With more businesses going online, safeguarding sensitive data and preventing cyberattacks is increasingly vital.

5. **Low-code development:** These platforms empower businesses to create software applications quickly and without extensive coding expertise.

6. **Superapps:** These combine multiple services into one platform, streamlining various tasks within a single app.

---

1   www.medium.com/geekculture/top-15-new-technology-trends-rule-the-2023-f25ddff23f5d, accessed September 11, 2023

7. **Applied observability:** This involves deep analysis of modern distributed systems, offering faster problem detection and resolution through real-time correlation of telemetry data.

8. **AI Trust Risk and Security Management (AI TRiSM):** AI TRiSM Ensuring AI operates securely, fairly, and effectively while protecting data and governance.

9. **Quantum computing:** This emerging technology promises faster and more memory-efficient computation, with applications in technology acceleration and encryption.

10. **Blockchain for Trust:** Blockchain technology, based on encryption, privacy, decentralization, and immutability, is gaining traction as a trust-building solution.

11. **Sustainable technology:** We can anticipate innovative digital solutions to support eco-friendly goals, optimize costs and improving energy efficiency.

12. **Wi-Fi 6 and 7:** These wireless network standards offer faster speeds, improved security, lower latency, and better support for various applications, from gaming to IoT.

Stay informed about these trends to remain at the forefront of technological advancements in 2024.

Cultivating a digital leader's mindset

I agree with Apoorva Chhabra, principal analyst at Gartner, who spotlights five behaviors that digital leaders are advised to adopt.[2] My comments are below each of her points.

1. **"Neophilia: A tendency to like anything new; a love of novelty"**

   The mindset of embracing innovation is key. Instead of considering what you already have, think about what you want to achieve.

2. **"Develop new opportunities: Invent, but also copy"**

   An eagle-eye view is key here. Look where you can best innovate, improvise, and copy before diving into your goals.

3. **"Pioneer new opportunities: Look beyond industry boundaries"**

   Effective digital leaders identify threats and opportunities that others wouldn't, which requires broad vision across markets. A pioneer in new opportunities embraces change within their industry while maintaining a clear vision of their industry's future.

---

2   A Chhabra, "How To Be A Successful Digital Transformation Leader" *CXOtoday*, (October 29 2022), www.cxotoday.com/cxo-bytes/ how-to-be-a-successful-digital-transformation-leader, accessed September 11, 2023

4. **"Seek new value-creation opportunities: Never consider digital to be the outcome"**

Before you invest in new digital technology, carefully examine the value proposition for your product or service, especially in regard to customer value and cost reduction.

Technology such as on-demand services, dynamic pricing, and real-time applications can strengthen your value proposition. However, if the results aren't tangible, the investment will not be worthwhile.

5. **"Focus on technology-driven opportunities: Geek out on technology"**

A technology-rich environment, where learning is encouraged, enabled, and expected. The more you democratize this knowledge, the more creative minds can contribute.

Strong business leaders are passionate about technology, which enables them to stay innovative and relevant in the marketplace. For example, in the culture created by ING's global CIO, ability to code is a must-have.

Effective digital leaders possess key characteristics such as a clear vision, and being innovative, collaborative, agile, customer-centric, data-driven, technologically savvy, empathetic, and results-orientated. If you want to up your game and become an exceptional leader, you will need to acquire the behavior that separates the good from the great. Truly great leaders have the following characteristics:

- They not only speak the language of their team and their clients but also focus on translating technology into value for the customer journey.

- They know why they are doing something and expect the same from their team, constantly testing the credibility of their team's motivation.

- They do not prejudge when there is cause for alarm but see this for themselves by *walking the gemba* (visiting the place where the work is carried out).

- They let their team shine and give them the credit they deserve.

- They are present, balancing the focus on now, next, and later.

- They make quick decisions to give their team a strong sense of direction.

Overall, great digital leaders prioritize human empowerment and use this to guide their daily business decisions.

HOW IT WORKS: The difference a great digital leader makes

A leading technology services company embarked on a digital transformation journey and hired Sarah Smit, a visionary executive known for her ability to harness the power of technology and drive meaningful value for customers.

Translating technology into value

Sarah understood that effective digital leaders not only speak the language of their team and clients but also focus on translating technology into value for the customer journey. She realized that the successful implementation of digital solutions required a deep understanding of customer needs and a relentless pursuit of delivering value. Sarah established a culture of innovation and customer-centricity, encouraging her team to view technology as an enabler in enhancing customer experiences. By aligning technology initiatives with customer demands, Sarah's team developed cutting-edge solutions that revolutionized the technology services industry.

Motivation and credibility

Sarah constantly tested the credibility of her team's motivation by fostering an environment of open communication and collaboration. She encouraged her team to challenge assumptions and contribute their unique perspectives. By nurturing an environment of trust and mutual respect, Sarah ensured that everyone was aligned with the company's vision and motivated to achieve the desired outcomes.

Walking the gemba

Sarah firmly believed in not prejudging and in seeing for herself when alarm signals arose. She engaged with her team members at all levels of the organization. This hands-on approach allowed her to gain firsthand insights into the challenges faced by her team and to identify opportunities for improvement. By actively listening and observing, Sarah demonstrated her commitment to understanding the ground reality and making informed decisions, based on accurate information.

Shining the spotlight on the team

As a great leader, Sarah understood the importance of giving credit where it was due. She acknowledged the contributions of her team and ensured that their achievements were recognized and celebrated. By creating a culture of appreciation and empowerment, Sarah motivated her team to excel, and she fostered a sense of pride and ownership in their work. This approach not only boosted morale but also nurtured a high-performing team, which consistently delivered exceptional results.

Balancing the now, next, and later

Sarah was a present leader, actively engaging with her team and the needs of the moment, and she understood the importance of balancing immediate priorities with long-term strategic goals. She recognized that focusing solely on the present might lead to missed opportunities for future growth, but that solely prioritizing the future could jeopardize the current success of the organization. Sarah skillfully balanced her attention between addressing immediate challenges, driving innovation for the future, and planning for long-term sustainability. Her ability to strike this delicate balance ensured that the business remained agile and well positioned to adapt to market changes.

Speedy decision-making and direction

Sarah recognized that, in a fast-paced digital landscape, delayed decision-making could hinder progress and demotivate her team. She made it a priority to make timely decisions and provide her team with a clear sense of direction. Sarah leveraged her deep understanding of the industry and market trends to swiftly evaluate options and make informed choices. By taking decisive action, she instilled confidence in her team, enabling them to move forward with purpose and clarity.

Human empowerment as a priority

Sarah prioritized human empowerment as the guiding principle behind her daily business decisions. She understood that technology alone could not drive sustainable success. By valuing her team members' unique skills and perspectives, Sarah created an inclusive environment that fostered creativity, collaboration, and growth. She championed professional development programs, mentoring initiatives, and employee wellbeing, ensuring that her team had the resources and support needed to thrive in the digital age.

Conclusion

Through Sarah's leadership, the company achieved remarkable success in their digital transformation journey. Sarah empowered her team to embrace change, drive innovation, and deliver exceptional value to customers. Her visionary approach and commitment to human empowerment set a new standard for digital leadership within the organization and inspired others to follow suit. With Sarah at the helm, the company became a trailblazer in the technology services industry, setting an example for companies aspiring to thrive in the digital era.

The power of visualization

Visualization is a tool that has been used by humans for centuries to turn ideas into reality. The power of visualization lies in its ability to transform abstract ideas into illustrations that can be seen and understood by others. It should be incorporated into every step of a company's strategy.

I used visualization to create and execute the plan for this book—see the figure on the next page.

As soon as an idea is visualized in 2D or 3D, it becomes tangible and easier to comprehend. Visualization creates a mental bridge between the idea and its execution, making it easier to turn abstract thoughts into concrete realities. It also enables others to understand ideas more easily, making it a powerful tool for transferring ideas.

Transformation as the cradle of innovation
RAPID Digital Transformation

Challenges
Agile/Dev Ops implementations
• Leadership
• Culture creep
• Strategy lives only in the boardroom
• No use of own talent in the company
• Losing touch with society
• Finance has a separate status in the company
• Innovation is something separate
• Why digital transformation fails

Problems
5-10 Mistakes

Method Step 1 Investigation	Method Step 2 Strategy	Method Step 3 Plan	Method Step 4 Transformation	Method Step 5 Operations
Exploring your situation	Building a successful digital strategy	Planning for success	Transforming your business into the new paradigm of digital	Running your business in a digitalized environment

Perfect reader: C-level, Change leads, Department heads, Business Coaches, Directors...
Control question: *What have I learned from this book?*
How to lead my (part of the) company into the new digital era.
For this I now have a simple model which helps me transform my (part of the) company.

My bookplan visualized in one of its early stages

Throughout this book, I will encourage you to explore and embrace the power of visualization to bring your ideas to life and to make them accessible to others. Visualization can transform your ideas into a reality that is not only visible but also easily understandable.

Summary

Great digital leaders:

- Are addicted to innovation but always seek value and tangible results for their customers and their business

- Keep up to speed with trends

- Take the eagle-eye view of threats and opportunities, now and in the future

- Are quick to give credit to their teams and are eager for their advancement, making sure they have the resources they need

- Above all, value humans above technology and often use visualization to share their ideas in a human-friendly way

2
Designing A Strategy For Success

Success is a complex phenomenon, which can be achieved through various strategies, while learning from failures is an equally important aspect of any pursuit. Success is achievable through careful planning, a willingness to take risks, and a commitment to continuous improvement.

Defining a clear strategy for success involves understanding the foundation principles that underpin any successful venture. Starting with the What is essential, while the How will emerge later as you begin to implement your plan.

Other key tools that can help you design a successful strategy include:

- Scenario thinking, which forces you to look from a range of perspectives

- The right platform, allowing for global scaling

- Action mindset, which is essential for strategy execution

- Sustainable architecture

- Effectiveness and efficiency

The What and the How

Defining a strategy for success is crucial when it comes to achieving your goals. It's important to start with the What and let the How naturally follow when moving to execution. There are times, however, when taking a different, additional approach can lead to even greater success.

I learned to always start with What early on in my career, when I was tasked with overseeing a project that had been dragging on for over a year. With no end in sight, the domain lead had come to me to vent his frustration. In my eagerness to solve the problem, and after studying the What by examining the current project details and asking the domain lead what he wanted to achieve, I confidently told him I could get the project finished within three months.

At first, I felt a rush of adrenaline at the prospect of taking on such a daunting challenge. As I started to dig into the details, though, I realized I had no concrete plan for how to achieve my What goal. I knew I needed to take a step back and reassess my approach.

Eliyahu M Goldratt's theory of constraints (TOC) came to my rescue. I spent the next few days rereading and rethinking his book *The Goal*, in which Goldratt maintains that organizations can achieve their goals by overcoming constraints.[3] I realized that, by focusing on the bottlenecks in the project and working to eliminate them, I could dramatically increase efficiency and get the project back on track. In the end, I was able to deliver on my promise and completed the project within three months.

The lesson I learned was not just about the power of the TOC; it was also about the importance of starting with the What and then being flexible enough to pivot when necessary. I also recognized that a crucial strategy for success is to think outside the box and try new things, even if they go against conventional wisdom. By combining a solid foundation with creativity and a willingness to experiment, you can achieve great things and overcome even the toughest challenges.

Scenario thinking

This involves assessing future threats and opportunities (scenarios) that could potentially change

---

3   EM Goldratt, *The Goal: A Process of Ongoing Improvement* (Gower, 1993)

the business landscape; choosing a year, preferably between three and seven years from the current time; and exploring different perspectives to determine the most likely outcomes of those scenarios. The goal is to identify the most uncertain areas, where opportunities can lead to paradigm shifts in terms of products and success. This method is used by many corporations such as Shell, which has been doing this since the oil crisis of the 1970s.[4]

The benefits of successful scenario thinking, especially with higher levels of foresight and pattern recognition, are depicted in the figure below.

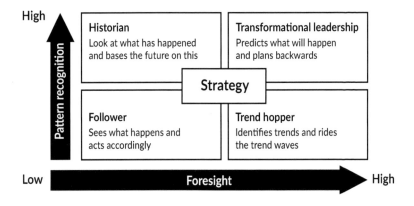

Scenario planning visualized

4   M Jefferson, "Shell scenarios: What really happened in the 1970s and what may be learned for current world prospects", *Technological Forecasting and Social Change*, 79/1 (2012), 186–197, www.sciencedirect.com/science/article/abs/pii/S0040162511001740, accessed September 11, 2023

There are five ingredients you should incorporate in scenario thinking:

1. Future factors that can possibly change reality

2. A year in the future (three to seven years ahead)

3. Questions to assess the future factors' likelihood and explore different perspectives

4. Writing a newspaper article about the scenario, dated in the future year you have selected

5. Five rules:

   - Be aware of bias

   - Define a relevant scope

   - Do not put your company name in the future scenario

   - Explore the area between conventional and absurd

   - Describe an event, not a trend

For any situation that you consider as a possibility but won't be included in your plan, you should set a point where it's too late to change your mind (meaning you can't switch to a different plan). This includes the points that make the situation seem realistic.

It's crucial to check on your alternative ideas regularly, like every quarter, and see if the reasons you have for your main plan are still valid. If you start to see signs that one of your backup plans might be a better choice, it's time to review your overall strategy. You can use an AI program to help you analyze these scenarios by feeding it the relevant information.

EXAMPLE: Scenario thinking

A tech company that specializes in creating virtual reality (VR) experiences want to expand their offerings and create a more immersive experience for customers.

Using scenario thinking, they decide to explore the idea of creating a VR theme park. They choose a year five years ahead and assess whether VR theme parks will be popular by then. They explore different perspectives such as the potential demand from customers and the feasibility of creating such an experience.

After voting on the most likely perspectives, they write a newspaper article set five years ahead, describing the opening of a VR theme park. The article describes the park's various attractions, including a roller coaster that takes customers on a virtual journey through space and a haunted house experience that feels eerily real.

While this scenario is exciting, they realize that it may not make it into their strategy. They define the point of no return for the VR theme park, including the costs and resources required to make it happen. They also look for signals that might make the scenario more realistic, such as an increase in demand for VR experiences.

As the company continues to grow and evolve, its strategists keep this scenario in mind and reassess it quarterly, to see if it becomes more relevant. Ultimately, scenario thinking helps them stay ahead of the curve and create innovative experiences their customers love.

The right platform

Foundational Technology Platforms, which enable users and technical staff to run and manage application software, have become the foundation for adding value to businesses. They offer scalability, network effects, and improved quality, among other benefits. Understanding the significance of platforms and their potential for adding value, including breaking inward-looking culture, is crucial for defining a successful strategy in today's global economy.

The right platform makes global scaling possible because innovation brings you instantly across borders, even if you are a niche player. Another purpose of thinking of global scaling is that you automatically do the math, for example, calculating what you need to do to scale ×100. Even answering this question will put you ahead of the game.

Defining a successful strategy therefore also entails choosing the right platform, which can be challenging, but it boils down to two choices: creating your own platform or using an existing one. If your focus is on value and your options are limited, using an existing platform is the way to go.

If you want to be a game changer, creating your own platform is a must, and this requires careful planning and preparation.

You have to prepare your company for platform development and make important architectural choices. Deploying a platform also involves defining clear governance and responsibilities, to achieve the desired business benefits and economies of scale, and monitoring implementation and adoption from the start. As businesses increasingly seek to expand their operations globally, they find that creating a global platform also requires the implementation of uniform processes. For example, when open banking was at an early stage, we decided to create an IT foundational platform (something like the Apple App Store) ourselves. To create the platform, we needed different engineering expertise on security, data transport, customer data, and frontend and microservices architecture, to build APIs (Application Programming Interface). Of course, we needed to manage this via lead architects, IT leads, road managers, and senior product owners to create a final platform usable in every country. In every country, they needed to adapt the platform specifications for use for third-party applications. In short, they needed to get ready to use our App Store.

As someone with five years of experience in developing a global platform and managing its rollout, I can attest that successful implementation of your own platform requires consistent visionary strategy, stamina, and persistence. After years of hard work and successfully initiating third-party payments (in compliance with PSD2 European regulations) via the ING platform across all the European countries where we had a presence, I was tasked with creating a rollout plan to increase adoption in Europe.

To achieve this, we created a dependency map, which we named the "Consumore map". It was inspired by the London Tube Map and showed, when read from left to right, how each step in the map made our platform more accessible for use, as shown over the page.

During our conversations with potential platform adopters, we realized it would be beneficial to have a heatmap indicating the adoption status of each country's basic features. This allowed us to focus our discussions and opportunities, according to the applicable country adoption and thereby scenarios.

To create healthy competition between countries, we color-coded each adopted feature in the Consumore map. This enabled us to visually track each country's adoption progress or chosen scenario and the according heatmap. This method was copied by several responsible CIOs—a measure of its success.

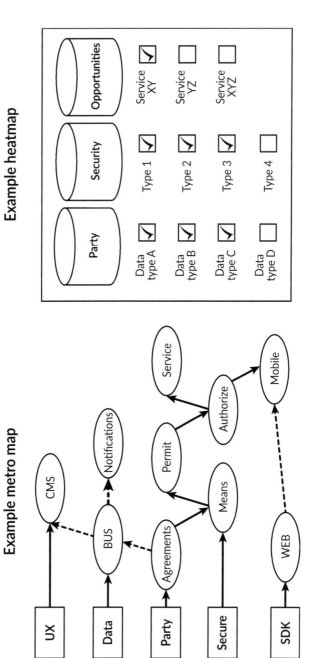

Example heatmap

Example metro map

Consumore map

Action mindset

During thirty years in business, I have seen many ideas fail during execution. I investigated what made ideas succeed, and based on this, I devised my action mindset.

Action mindset: Essential for successful strategy execution

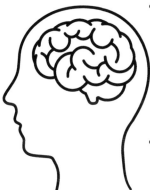

- Creating a better tomorrow
  - Engagement for productivity
    - Leveraging talent within
      - Starting a movement
        - Innovation through controlled unbalance
        - Communication triangle with confidants
        - Change portfolio assessment
        - Focus on the goal
      - Law of urgency
    - Operational optimization
  - Personal attitude
- Follow the RAPID Digital Transformation Model

A certain mindset, in addition to leadership qualities, is crucial to success in implementing strategies. Here are the essential components of the action mindset, as shown above.

- **Creating a better tomorrow**

  It is important to take actions today that will create a better starting point for tomorrow.

- **Engagement for productivity**

  Leaders should connect with their team members to create a productive work environment. Engaged employees are more productive.

- **Leveraging talent within**

  Leaders should look beyond job descriptions and appreciate the unique skills and experiences of their employees. Asking for their help not only helps solve challenges but also engages employees.

- **Starting a movement**

  Building collaborative communities is vital to growing expertise. Collaboration fosters engagement and creates a platform for sharing ideas and knowledge.

- **Innovation through controlled unbalance**

  Leaders should introduce just enough change to stimulate creativity without disrupting the entire system.

- **Communication triangle with confidants**

  Leaders should establish confidants in critical layers of the organization. Confidants are individuals who have the trust of their peers and can provide valuable insights and feedback. By including confidants in the communication triangle, leaders can ensure that information about the strategy execution status flows smoothly throughout the organization. This improves alignment and collaboration, as well as increases the likelihood of successful strategy implementation. You will find more examples of this in Part Two, where I take you through my RAPID Digital Transformation Model.

- **Change portfolio assessment**

  Leaders should regularly have their change portfolio assessed from an external perspective. This eliminates organizational blindness and identifies areas that need improvement.

- **Focus on the goal**

  Leaders should avoid politics and focus on the end goal. They should have a flexible plan that accommodates changes and a PDCA—plan, do, check, act— cycle (Deming Cycle),[5] for continuous improvement.

- **Law of urgency**

  Procrastination is the enemy of progress. Leaders should move quickly to achieve their goals.

- **Operational optimization**

  Leaders should have their operational and change processes assessed by either a Six Sigma Black Belt, using a DMAIC (define, measure, analyze, improve, control) toolbox[6] and / or an equivalent such as a Lean Black Belt (using the Lean House principles).[7]

---

5   K Feldman, "How PDCA can help improve organizational efficiency", (iSixSigma, 2023), www.isixsigma.com / dictionary / deming-cycle-pdca, accessed September 12, 2023

6   M Uluskan, "A comprehensive insight into the Six Sigma DMAIC toolbox", *International Journal of Lean Six Sigma*, 7 / 4 (2016), 406–429, www.emerald.com / insight / content / doi / 10.1108 / IJLSS-10-2015-0040 / full / html

7   M Brenig-Jones and J Dowdall, *Learn Six Sigmas for Dummies*, 4th edition (For Dummies, 2021)

- **Personal attitude**

  In addition to the action mindset qualities, personal attitude is critical for success. Leaders should observe first, begin if they believe in the cause, stay in contact with themselves, listen to their intuition, and choose a way to progress.

- **Follow the RAPID Digital Transformation Model**

  This sets the base to get the critical 20% in place so that 80% of work will be successful. The RAPID Digital Transformation Model will be explained in detail in Part Two.

Sustainable architecture

Before delving into the key elements of a sustainable IT architecture, it's essential to emphasize the importance of effectively communicating the architectural message. While architects may be passionate about their profession and dedicated to serving the company's best interests, conveying their ideas to non-technical stakeholders can be challenging.

To overcome this hurdle, architects can create explanatory slides with simple, easy-to-understand panels that outline how the IT landscape is tied together. These slides can be used to facilitate solution discussions, providing a clear understanding of the What while also explaining the How.

There are five crucial elements that should be included in a sustainable IT architecture:

1. **Scalability:** To ensure longevity and effectiveness, a robust IT architecture is scalable—capable of adapting to changing business needs and handling increasing amounts of data and traffic—without sacrificing performance or stability.

2. **Flexibility:** A robust IT architecture is also flexible—able to integrate with different systems and technologies—to take advantage of new opportunities and innovations without requiring a complete overhaul of the IT infrastructure.

3. **Security:** Security is paramount, and a robust IT architecture is designed with security measures in mind to protect against cyber threats, data breaches, and other security risks.

4. **Resilience:** A robust IT architecture is resilient, capable of recovering quickly from disruptions or failures. This involves implementing redundancy measures to ensure that critical systems and data are always available, even in the event of a disaster or outage.

5. **Sustainability:** Finally, a robust IT architecture is designed with sustainability in mind. This includes implementing energy-efficient technologies and practices like virtualization and cloud computing to reduce energy consumption and carbon footprint.

By considering these elements and designing an architecture that is scalable, flexible, secure, resilient, and sustainable, businesses can build a robust IT architecture that can support their needs for years to come.

Effectiveness and efficiency

Achieving effectiveness and efficiency in a global company setting can be challenging.

Imagine a global corporation with multiple offices around the world. Each office operates independently, with its own set of procedures and technologies, making it difficult to achieve standardization and efficiency across the organization. The company therefore hires a team of consultants to streamline its operations and create a global IT architecture that could support all its offices.

The team spends months analyzing data, conducting interviews, and devising strategies to unify the company's operations and technologies. However, when the new plan is presented, the team encounters resistance. Some offices feel that the new procedures will disrupt their current workflows, while others argue that their technology is superior to what is being proposed. The consultants have overlooked the importance of engaging with the stakeholders from the start.

To overcome this resistance and get everyone on board with the new plan, the consultants launch a series of workshops that bring together representatives from each office, to discuss their concerns and generate solutions. Over several months, the workshops help build trust and consensus among the various stakeholders until, eventually, the new plan can be implemented.

The new architecture leads to greater standardization, improved collaboration, and increased efficiency across the organization. However, the success of the project is not guaranteed in the long term. To truly achieve effectiveness and efficiency, the consultants would have needed to recommend a full culture change program throughout the organization, to set an innovation culture, and to create an environment where people would stay to enjoy even more rewarding work.

The company needs to be open and honest about its goal setting and motivation to create a sustainable future. Everyone needs to be offered a way forward to success. That might even require some employees moving to a different company if they are unable to adapt to the new changes.

In this way, the company could create *effectiveness*. This would in turn increase *efficiency* by ensuring that:

- Employees are willing to support the company's next steps

- The accounting team within the financial department sees a more realistic and efficient path laid out

- The company prospers thanks to the clarity it shows to society and its stakeholders

Summary

To design a strategy for success:

- You should start with What but be flexible enough to pivot when necessary.

- Scenario thinking forces you into perspectives beyond your own.

- Creating your own robust architecture, if possible, is the way to be a game changer, but you must communicate well from the start.

- If you don't have the means to create your own, reuse someone else's platform.

- The mindset necessary for execution emphasizes the importance of awareness and a *just do it* mentality.

- Conveyable messaging, and a focus on effectivity and efficiency, are key to a successful architecture.

PART TWO
THE RAPID SOLUTION

Wisdom and success can only be
triggered from within.

3

Introducing
The RAPID Digital
Transformation Model

The RAPID Digital Transformation Model is a simple and effective guide for every phase of your transformation journey. It's my version of the 80/20 rule, which stresses the importance of getting the 20% foundation right so as not to waste 80% of the investment or work attached to it.

Each of the model's five phases has its success formula, which can be easily remembered via the RAPID pointer—see the next page. The arrows below illustrate that the RAPID iterates and goes back and forth.

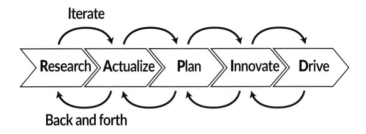

RAPID pointer

In this chapter I'll introduce you to the RAPID Digital Transformation Model, explain when and how to use it, and provide key starting points for effective implementation. I'll also share my experiences on how to predict success or failure in transformation initiatives by observing the buzz around a program and how it is introduced.

By the end of this chapter, you'll have:

- A deep understanding of the RAPID Digital Transformation Model and its various phases

- A roadmap for successful implementation, as well as insights on how to predict success or failure in your transformation initiatives

- Knowledge of how to run your operation in a digital-native way

RAPID Digital Transformation Model overview

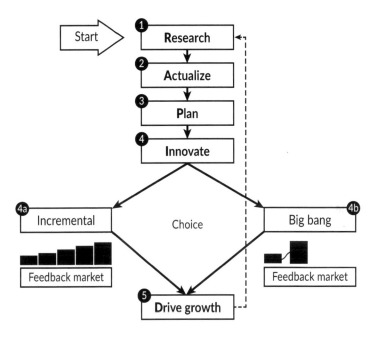

RAPID Digital Transformation Model illustration

1. **R: Research your market**

   Exploring your situation to determine your (IT) strategy

2. **A: Actualize your digital strategy**

   Building a successful, executable digital strategy; making it real

3. **P: Plan for success**

   Anticipating hurdles with a realistic plan

4. **I: Innovate through transformation**

   Transforming your business into the new paradigm of digital

5. **D: Drive growth**

   Running your business in a digital environment

Understand the model constraints

The RAPID Digital Transformation Model is ideal for companies determining transformation initiatives where digitization is a key aspect, but it can also be applied in a broader sense. It may not be the best fit for projects smaller than one million euros (approximately £860,000 at the time of writing), as the model may be too extensive. However, in these cases it can still be used as a guide.

You can use the model effectively for the transformation of a company department or nonprofit-sector department, focusing on each phase as if the department were a complete company. However, it's important to be aware that you are only one of the many gears within the larger organization or nonprofit sector, so it's crucial to consider how the departmental initiative fits into the bigger picture. Starting at the A of the model (Actualize your digital strategy) can be a good approach in these cases because the company strategy as a whole is, in most cases, already defined.

To increase the chances of success for any transformation initiative, including those that use the RAPID Digital Transformation Model, it's important to have a clear understanding of the need for transformation, strong leadership and commitment, openness to change, adequate resources, and clear communication.

The power of simplicity in change initiatives

Simplicity is a critical factor in the success of change initiatives. As a CIO, you understand that change is often met with resistance, especially when people are comfortable with the status quo and fail to see the need for change. By transforming difficult and complex change into smaller increments, you can keep things simple and easy to understand, thereby reducing resistance and increasing buy-in from stakeholders.

Keeping change initiatives simple can also help increase clarity and understanding of what needs to be done. When things are complex or difficult to understand, confusion and lack of clarity will hinder progress. It is important to prioritize simplicity in all aspects of your change initiatives.

Furthermore, simplicity helps with implementation. When a change initiative is simple, it is typically easier to implement and manage, which reduces the likelihood of issues and delays. This can lead to faster progress and greater success, enabling you to achieve your goals more effectively.

In summary, simplicity helps increase clarity, reduce resistance, and aid implementation, all of which are key factors in the success of change initiatives.

Start with Why and What

While Start with Why[8] is a well-known concept, popularized by Simon Sinek, when it comes to transformation initiatives, it's important to follow the Why with What. Starting with Why helps create a sense of purpose and motivation for change, but it's equally important to clearly define what the transformation entails. Without a clear understanding of what needs to be changed, it is difficult to create a plan of action or communicate the transformation to stakeholders.

By starting with Why and then immediately moving to What, we will create a clear picture of the transformation and the desired outcomes. This will help to align everyone involved toward a common goal and enable effective planning and execution.

Without a clear understanding of the purpose behind the change (Why) and a well-defined plan for implementation (What), organizations risk

---

8   S Sinek, *Start With Why: How great leaders inspire everyone to take action* (Portfolio, 2009)

encountering challenges and limited success in their transformation efforts.

Here are two examples—one good practice and one not so good.

EXAMPLE: Do it like this

A retail chain had been experiencing declining sales due to increased competition from online retailers. The company decided to launch a transformation initiative, with the goal of creating a seamless omnichannel experience for customers.

Starting with Why, they communicated to employees and stakeholders that the transformation was necessary to meet changing customer needs and remain competitive in the marketplace. The company emphasized that the goal was not just to increase sales but also to create a better experience for customers, regardless of whether they shopped online or in-store.

Moving to What, several key areas were identified that needed to be addressed to achieve the desired outcomes of the transformation. These included:

- Implementing a new inventory management system to ensure accurate and timely stock updates across all channels
- Developing a mobile app to allow customers to easily find products, check availability, and place orders
- Upgrading the company's website to improve user experience and increase online sales

- Redesigning physical stores to make them more inviting and interactive, with features like digital kiosks and product demonstrations

Those leading the changes engaged with employees at all levels of the organization and provided training and support to help them adapt to the changes. The company also communicated regularly with customers to gather feedback on the transformation and made adjustments as needed.

As a result of the transformation, the company saw a significant increase in sales and customer satisfaction. Their online sales grew by 30%, and in-store sales also increased due to the improved in-store experience. Customer feedback was overwhelmingly positive, with many praising the new omnichannel capabilities and the company's focus on creating a better customer experience.

In conclusion, by starting with Why and moving to What, it was possible to successfully implement a transformation initiative that addressed a key business challenge and created real value for customers. By clearly defining the desired outcomes and engaging employees and customers throughout the process, the company was able to achieve its goals and remain competitive in the marketplace.

EXAMPLE: Not like this

A manufacturing firm decided to embark on a transformation journey without a clear understanding of the Why and What aspects of their initiative.

The leadership recognized the need for change, to improve operational efficiency and reduce costs. However, they failed to effectively communicate the Why behind the transformation to their employees and stakeholders. As a result, there was a lack of clarity and sense of purpose among the workforce, leading to resistance and skepticism.

The company's approach to defining the What of the transformation was equally flawed. Instead of identifying specific areas for improvement and setting clear objectives, they implemented a series of scattered and disconnected changes.

They introduced new software systems without proper integration, changed processes without considering the impact on employee workflows, and made organizational restructuring decisions without a well-defined strategy.

Without a clear understanding of what needed to be changed and how it would align with the company's overall goals, the transformation initiative resulted in confusion, inefficiency, and a loss of productivity. Employees struggled to adapt to the changes, leading to a decline in morale and a decrease in overall performance.

Furthermore, the lack of a cohesive plan and effective communication resulted in a loss of trust in the company and damaged relationships with key business partners.

In the end, the transformation fell short of its intended outcomes. Operational efficiency did not improve, costs remained high, and the company's competitive position weakened. The lack of a clear Why and What, combined with poor execution, led to a failed transformation that left the organization in a worse state than before.

Summary

The RAPID Digital Transformation Model is a simple and effective guide for your transformation journey. When using this model, remember:

- Keeping things simple adds clarity, reduces resistance, and makes implementation easier.

- Why without What has no meaning for stakeholders.

With this in mind, let's delve into the RAPID Digital Transformation Model itself in the next chapters, where we will go through each phase: Research your market, Actualize your digital strategy, Plan for success, Innovate through transformation, and Drive growth.

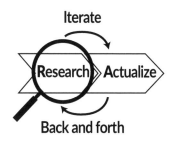

Iterate

Research ⟩ Actualize

Back and forth

4

RAPID Phase 1: Research Your Market

As businesses and organizations continue to navigate the ever-evolving digital landscape, it has become increasingly important to have a solid digital strategy in place.

In the Research phase of your transformation journey, defining your strategy and developing a compelling story behind that strategy are crucial to your success. This step is akin to music—starting on the wrong note can make it challenging to get back in tune.

To achieve success, it's essential to understand five golden rules:

Rule 1: Do not engage too soon with an external consultancy partner (or even a strategy partner).

Rule 2: Do not try to invent expertise that you don't have in-house.

Rule 3: As soon as you engage with a consultancy partner, ensure that your collaboration is time-limited.

Rule 4: The consultancy partner should understand and apply your narrative, not the other way around.

Rule 5: Test the outcome of this Research phase with trusted colleagues within your organization.

Strategize your ambitions

As a CIO, you may face the challenge of developing a business/IT strategy. Here are five steps that will help you overcome potential difficulties:

1. Establish a clear vision of what you want to achieve and the goals you want to accomplish.

2. Conduct a SWOT (strengths, weaknesses, opportunities, threats) analysis to match your goals and capabilities with your environment.[9]

3. Determine your customer segments and their needs and expectations, and tailor your strategy accordingly.

---

9   J Bos and E Harting, *Creative Project Management 2.0* (Scriptum, 2006)

4. Ensure your IT strategy aligns with your overall business strategy and prioritize your initiatives accordingly.

5. Use tools such as the business model canvas, developed by Alex Osterwalder,[10] to identify the key building blocks of your business model. These blocks include the value proposition, customer segments, channels, customer relationships, revenue streams, key resources, key activities, key partnerships, cost structure, and societal and environmental benefits/costs.

The Business Model Canvas

The Business Model Canvas is one example of a tool you can use to develop a strategy for your company. An adapted version of Osterwalder's original can be downloaded from the Business Models Inc. website.[11] Whatever the nature of your business, the canvas allows you to prioritize your initiatives and allocate your resources accordingly, ensuring that you deliver value to your customers while remaining profitable. Here are some tips on populating your Business Model Canvas using an example of a cloud-based project management tool for a software company.

---

10 A Osterwalder, "What is a business model?", (Strategyzer, no date), www.strategyzer.com/library/what-is-a-business-model, accessed September 15, 2023

11 Business Models Inc., "Business model canvas", www.businessmodelsinc.com/en/inspiration/tools/business-model-canvas, accessed September 17, 2023

HOW IT WORKS: Populating your business model canvas using the example of a cloud-based project management tool.

Key partners. These are all the partners (not suppliers) essential to your business. They could be technology companies that can integrate your software with other tools.

Examples:

- Cloud Service Providers: ensuring reliable and scalable hosting
- Integration partners: collaborating with other software providers to enhance functionality

Key activities. These are the daily activities required by your business model and may include software development, customer acquisition, and customer support.

Examples:

- Software development and maintenance: building and updating the cloud-based project management tool
- User experience design: ensuring a user-friendly and efficient tool interface

Key resources. These include everything you need to run your business – your employees, expertise, and finance.

Examples:

- Technology infrastructure: cloud servers and development resources
- Software engineers: expertise for developing and maintaining the tool

Value propositions. These are your products and services – list everything your company provides for its customers.

Example:

- Cloud-Based Project Management Tool: Offers an intuitive and collaborative tool for efficient project planning, tracking, and communication

Customer relationships. How you manage these can take different forms – list everything your business does to maintain customer relationships.

Example:

- Customer support: offering responsive customer support to address queries and issues

Channels. These are the ways in which you communicate with and deliver to your customers.

Examples:

- Online marketing: leveraging digital marketing channels to reach potential customers
- Website and app: providing easy access for customers

Customer segments. These are the future segments to focus on – those that are likely to provide the most revenue.

Example:

- Small and medium enterprises looking for efficient project management solutions

Cost structure. This includes all costs related to your activities and resources.

Examples:

- Development costs: investments in software development and updates
- Cloud hosting fees: costs associated with using cloud servers
- Personnel costs: salaries for software engineers and support staff

Revenue streams—your main revenue sources

List all the main streams of income for your business.

Example:

- Subscription fees: charges for customers to use your cloud-based project management tool

Societal and environmental costs. Include here any negative impacts of your business model, for example societal and environmental effects.

Examples:

- Energy consumption: consideration of energy used for running servers and infrastructure
- Carbon footprint: monitoring and mitigating carbon emissions related to data centers
- Data privacy concerns: addressing potential societal concerns related to date security and privacy

Societal and environmental benefits. The positive impacts of your business model include any measures you take to counteract societal and environmental costs.

Examples:

- Remote work facilitation: contributing to work-life balance
- Enhancing project efficiency: leading to reduced stress and better job satisfaction
- Paperless operations: reducing paper usage and carbon footprint
- Remote access: allowing teams to collaborate from different locations, reducing the need for travel

---

Write your own story before you bring in consultants

Remember Rule 1: do not engage too soon with external consultants. Every company and department has its unique success story, which should not be compromised by bringing in outsiders to write the narrative.

During my time in the semi-public sector, my organization was suffering from organizational changes, which contributed to declining results. An external consultant who lacked expertise and experience in our field presented a standard solution, stating that he had already seen our situation a dozen times before. This approach left us feeling undervalued and frustrated, and the consultant was dismissed the following day.

It is important to adhere to your company's unique identity. You should ensure that your narrative is crafted by your team, no matter how radical the paradigm shift needs to be. It is essential to test the outcome of your Research phase with people you trust within your organization, to ensure the ideal starting point is defined by you and your team. This is crucial to maintaining your own company identity now, and in the future, and it is a vital part of your success.

With Rule 1 in mind, we move on to Rule 2: do not try to invent expertise that you don't have in-house. When you have determined the starting points of your ambition, it is time to hire an external consultancy firm (or craft a strategic alliance). Preferably, select a top-notch consultancy firm such as McKinsey, BCG, or Accenture, all of which have crafted countless strategy papers and translated them into shareholder-proof stories.

The consultants can calculate the overall business case and set strategy in motion, and they will leave after your own people have learned and adopted the new story, ready to take it forward to completion. In this way, you also adhere to Rule 3: ensuring that your collaboration with the consultancy is time-limited and that you can separate easily.

EXAMPLE: Do it like this

A company's board had a vision to expand their market share by investing in new technology and digital transformation. They decided to hire a well-known consultancy firm to develop a comprehensive strategy and business case to present to their stakeholders.

The consultancy firm worked closely with the board and identified several areas for improvement, including revamping their website, creating a mobile app, and implementing a customer relationship management (CRM) system. They also analyzed the market and identified new opportunities for growth such as expanding into new geographic markets.

The consultancy firm presented the strategy and business case to the stakeholders, who were impressed with the plan and approved the budget for implementation. The consultancy firm then conducted internal training sessions to ensure that the employees understood the new strategy and were equipped to implement it.

Once the consultancy firm completed their work, the company took over implementation. They created an execution plan including cultural changes and assigned resources to ensure that the plan was executed successfully. The company was able to successfully implement the new technology, and within a year, they saw an increase in revenue and market share.

Although the consultancy firm was not involved in the execution phase, their guidance and expertise were instrumental in helping the company develop a concrete plan to achieve their vision. By working with the consultancy firm, the company was able to ensure their strategy was well thought out and aligned with their overall business goals.

Understand your company's narrative

Here comes Rule 4: The external consultant should understand and apply your narrative, not the other way around. Before giving an assignment to a consultancy firm, it's important to have clear expectations and to know what you're looking for. Here are some steps you can take to ensure you're choosing the right consultancy firm:

1. **Define your problem:** Before approaching a consultancy firm, define the problem you want to solve. This will help you identify the type of consultancy firm that can best help you. The same applies with a strategic alliance.

2. **Research potential firms:** Look for consultancy firms that have experience in your industry and have solved similar problems. Check their websites, case studies, and online reviews to get a sense of their expertise.

3. **Think outside the box when necessary:** If you are looking for a real paradigm shift, look at firms who understand your business but who can advise their clients in different directions. You will need to employ intuition here, to judge each consultancy's versatility and breadth of experience.

4. **Check their credentials:** Ensure the consultancy firm has the necessary credentials and certifications to provide the services you need.

5. **Understand their methodology:** Consultancy firms have different approaches to problem-solving. Determine which firms' approaches align with your expectations and preferences.

6. **Communicate your expectations:** Clearly communicate your expectations and goals to the consultancy firm. This will help them tailor their approach to your needs and ensure they deliver the desired results.

By following these steps, you can find the consultancy firm that is best suited to meet your expectations and solve your problem. Before formalizing any agreement, however, apply Rule 5: Test the outcome of this Research phase with trusted colleagues within your organization.

Get ready to drive execution yourself

Once you have selected your external advisers, you need to get your own employees ready for taking over after the consultancy phase. People who strategize and those who deliver and make a strategy executable are different breeds. Handing over the execution of a program from a consultancy firm to internal teams can therefore be a complex process.

Here is how you can have confidence in its success.

- **Knowledge transfer:** Ensure the consultancy firm provides a comprehensive knowledge-transfer process to the internal teams. This includes documentation, training, and mentorship to ensure that the internal teams have a thorough understanding of the program and can effectively execute it.

- **Clearly defined roles and responsibilities:** The roles and responsibilities of both the consultancy firm and internal teams should be clearly defined. This ensures there is no confusion about what each party is responsible for and accountable for.

- **Robust project management:** Ensure there is robust project management process in place on both sides, and that both sides collaborate on managing the handover process. This includes regular check-ins, progress reports, and tracking of deliverables.

- **Knowledge retention:** Ensure your internal teams have a clear plan for how to retain the knowledge gained during the engagement with the consultancy firm. This plan includes documentation and training for new team members, and a process for continuous improvement, to ensure the program remains effective over time.

- **Continuous support:** Ensure the consultancy firm provides ongoing support during the handover process and beyond. This includes regular check-ins, troubleshooting, and support for any issues that arise during the execution phase.

If all these elements are in place, you can expect the handover process to be smooth and effective, and the internal teams will be well equipped to execute the program successfully.

Summary

By following the five golden rules of the Research phase and the other steps in this chapter, you can:

- Strategize your ambitions

- Understand your company narrative

- Select consultancy firms or strategic partners that understand and apply your narrative

- Prepare your own team from the start, ensuring successful handover of the new strategy

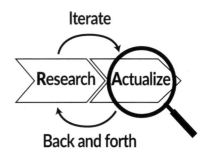

5

RAPID Phase 2: Actualize Your Digital Strategy

A digital strategy can help organizations stay competitive, improve customer experience, and drive growth. However, acquiring a strategy is only the first step; the real challenge lies in actualizing or executing that strategy effectively.

Actualizing digital strategy involves translating ideas into action, implementing technologies and processes, and ensuring that the strategy is aligned with overall business goals. It requires collaboration across departments, a focus on continuous improvement, and the ability to adapt to changing circumstances. You are like the captain of a ship, navigating toward transformational success.

The Actualize phase of the RAPID digital strategy framework takes the strategic plan and makes it a reality, through effective implementation, monitoring, and refinement. In this chapter we will explore the key elements of actualizing digital strategy and provide insights on how to ensure successful execution. Before proceeding, I recommend taking a moment to consider the creation of an innovative culture. While some may argue that innovation should be a fundamental part of defining a strategy, I believe it primarily resides in the preparation for execution. Innovation is not something that can be summoned on demand; it requires the right cultural foundation. I will therefore begin this chapter by addressing how to create that foundation, after which I will delve into the elements of actualization.

Foster an innovation culture

As an experienced change agent aware of the frame I operate in, I like to step out of the frame from time to time. This allows me to see how I can play with it from the eagle-eye perspective, to better understand the phenomenon of change.

An intriguing question that occupied me during this process: How do some companies continue to innovate successfully? The answer is simple: Innovation is normally nothing more than striving for the restoration of a lost balance. This perhaps provocative statement also explains why some companies stay on top, and others disappear because they have lost the innovation culture.

Innovation is a key component of success for businesses, and understanding the hidden definition of innovation is essential to achieve it. One pattern or law that can be observed in change initiatives is that they are always sparked by a disruption or imbalance in the system. When a business is taken out of its comfort zone, the natural human impulse is to restore balance as quickly as possible to regain a sense of safety and security.

Companies that can continuously innovate and remain successful do so by following three key strategies.

1. Constantly renewing strategies

This is demonstrated in political initiatives, like those surrounding the climate and energy transition. Legislation is continuously adapting, encouraging businesses to change their behavior while still maintaining control of their operations by having their employees innovating the processes to adapt to the new reality, even in the face of changing regulations. When regulations change, consumers and businesses suddenly find themselves outside the norm, and their natural inclination is to adapt to these changes, to achieve a status quo or even improve their situation.

The banking industry is another example of how changing regulations can lead to innovation. When PSD2 legislation was introduced, it prompted innovation within the banking sector, including the development of new services and increased digitalization. ING used this momentum to develop and launch its new platform, which provided a one-stop solution for all PSD2-related services for both ING's own customers and third parties across multiple countries, simplifying the connection for third parties across borders.

Changes to rules and regulations create an imbalance that triggers a natural compensatory reaction, which leads to innovation. Since the starting point has changed, it cannot be restored by returning to the old ways, so some degree of innovation will always be necessary to achieve the former status quo, or even improve on it.

2. Increasing the diversity of their teams

Companies with a culture of innovation intentionally create a different team dynamic that seeks to achieve the status quo or better. When old patterns of leadership or team dynamics no longer work, diverse teams search for new challenges and tasks they can take on.

3. Mastering the situation

Once leaders have introduced just enough disruption, the perfect starting conditions are met for companies to use innovation to master their situation. There are three main elements of successful innovation:

- **Painting a compelling picture of the future** helps counteract the feelings of insecurity that arise from the initial disruption.

- **Creating urgency** is crucial because the first company to innovate and materialize this vision will likely become the new market leader.

- **Creating space for experimentation and learning** is essential because innovation is often an iterative process that involves trial and error, or in Agile terms: *Fail fast, learn fast.*[12]

Align internal stakeholders

One of the key challenges of actualization is ensuring that all stakeholders within an organization are in agreement with and committed to the strategy execution. This is critical for the successful execution of the strategy, as it ensures that all employees are working toward a common goal and understand the importance of their roles in achieving it. As CIO or digital lead, you should appoint an overall program lead who can select a team to ensure that all stakeholders are aligned and committed to the successful execution

---

12 R Goldberg and J Ruehlin, "Fail fast and learn fast" (IBM, no date) www.ibm.com/garage/method/practices/culture/failing-fast, accessed September 18, 2023

of the digital strategy. The following points will help that team achieve this alignment:

- Communication is critical to achieving alignment across all levels of the organization. Once you have completed the Research and Strategy phases, take the time to communicate your strategy throughout the organization. This involves a comprehensive plan for communication, including townhall sessions, visiting workers on the floor, engaging in coffee-corner conversations, and having consulting with employees over lunch.

- Leverage your trusted employees—your confidants—to help spread the word and encourage colleagues to embrace the digital strategy.

- Be open to feedback and willing to adjust your plans accordingly. This feedback can come from stakeholders at any level of the organization, all of whom have valuable insights to offer.

- Line up the management team who will execute and take over from the external consultancy firm. The business lead needs to be mandated to take decisions where needed and make sure that business tradeoffs are made in time, without delaying the IT strategy implementation.

- Prioritize the digital strategy in relation to other ongoing initiatives and provide regular updates on progress.

These steps will ensure that all stakeholders are aligned and committed to the successful execution of the digital strategy and that your organization is well positioned to embrace the opportunities presented by the digital landscape.

Communicate for success

Communication is key when it comes to executing your digital strategy. To communicate effectively, you should start by translating your strategy narrative into real-life examples that are aligned with your company's values and can resonate with your coworkers.

Top-level managment	Strategy narrative	Communicating the vision
Middle management		Setting functional goals
Functional management		Cross integration of strategies
Front-line management		Cascade goals into daily operations
Operational employees		Adaptation and task execution
Feedback		

Overview of how your message can translate into the different organization layers

When the CEO of ING shared his digital strategy in 2013, he sparked the beginning of an exciting transformation program. The program focused on three critical themes: *people, process,* and *technology,* each with their own unique challenges to overcome.

1. **People:** The ING team introduced the Dreyfus model of skill acquisition[13], which ensured high-performing teams working collaboratively toward their goals.

2. **Process:** This was all about transforming the way of work within ING Netherlands, while also paving the way for a global way of work based on the Agile DevOps approach.

3. **Technology:** Here the team focused on phasing out legacy systems and simplifying their technological landscape. For example, they implemented a renewed datacenter strategy and decided to phase out the mainframe in favor of a microservice architecture.

I was the program lead and worked closely with the program director, who managed our executives and stakeholders. My team had to define its execution strategy and make changes along the way. One significant change was replacing the initial consultancy firm, which conducted strategy support, with a more execution-driven firm, to help us achieve our goals with us in the driving seat.

---

13 The Dreyfus Model of Skill Acquisition was developed by Stuart and Hubert Dreyfus in 1980 as part of their research at the University of California.

With the global CIO/CTO involved, the new team held weekly progress meetings with all CIOs of the different technology lines and their direct reports. This strong communication strategy also included the chief of communications within IT, who coordinated events, newsletters, interviews, infographics, videos, and everything else that supported the transformation program. Together, we drove the program forward, and our peers within the organization were motivated on a weekly basis, making for an exciting and dynamic time at ING.

To play my part, I had to be a good communicator. Effective communication is crucial for successful innovation management and transformation processes. Many individuals struggle with communication due to factors such as speech anxiety and being frequently misunderstood. Two other common challenges when speaking are physical stress and the voice in your head questioning the relevance or interest of your message. Remember:

- Everyone has their own perspective, which means that your perspective always adds value to theirs.

- Simplicity in messaging is key.

- Adding storytelling to engage your audience makes the message more appetizing.

Communication tips

According to research, approximately 70% of the message is carried through **non-verbal communication**.[14] I believe this is true during physical engagement, as our attention span is limited. If you can interpret someone's posture, and combine that with their opening statements, you will already have a good idea of what's coming next.

It is therefore important to consider the following when you are talking:

- **Facial expressions:** Support your message with the right facial expressions. If you're telling a joke, it really helps if you also smile. Conversely, when delivering a serious message, nervous laughter works counterproductively.

- **Hands:** Your hands and gestures often tell a story, so ensure they are congruent with what you are saying.

- **Body posture:** When you're in the company of a few people, pay attention to the body posture of others. Are they copying your posture as a speaker, or are they doing the opposite? If it's the opposite, is their posture open (for example, with relaxed shoulders) or closed (for example,

---

14 RL Birdwhistell, "Implications of Recent Developments in Communication Research for Evolutionary Theory", in WM Austin (ed.), *Report of the Ninth Annual Round Table Meeting on Linguistics and Language Study* (Georgetown University Press, 1960), 149–155

crossed arms)? If their posture is closed, your message might not be accepted outright. It might then be a good idea to invest some time in understanding others before pushing your own story.

Verbal communication can be enhanced by understanding the four communication styles: content, process, relationship, and emotion. Recognizing the style and connecting to it will enhance connection in communication. Listening, summarizing, and digging deeper (LSD) are also essential tools for effective conversation.

For **written communication**, I recommend using the Pyramid Principle to create a logical and persuasive structure.[15] The abbreviation I always use is SCQA—situation, context, question, answer. Connecting it to your source, you start with sketching the situation, your viewpoint supported by analysis, and the proposed next steps. You can of course vary the order; sometimes you want to end with a question, and sometimes there is an imaginative question you already answer in your context or situation description.

Finally, when it comes to **public speaking**, make the story your own, focus on a few key points, leverage storytelling, and incorporate interactive elements.

---

15 B Minto, *The Pyramid Principle: Logic in writing and thinking* (Pitman, 1991)

By applying these tips, you can improve your communication skills and enhance the success of your transformation initiatives.

Flying solo

Setting yourself up for success without relying on contractors is a critical step toward independence and self-reliance. As you near the end of the Actualize phase, it's essential to take a strategic approach to managing your time, resources, and investments. At this point, the consultancy firm can retreat and step back into monitoring mode, allowing you to take the lead.

To start, let's focus on investment. Although you have already conducted research, there might be changes now that you have collected feedback and recruited the program lead. Consider enlisting the help of a financial controller or adviser to help you manage your finances and make informed decisions about how to invest your resources. A financial expert can provide guidance on market trends, identify potential risks and opportunities, develop financial models and forecasts, and design customized financial solutions that align with your goals and objectives.

It's also essential to take a broad view of your resources. Consider technology, machines, outsourcing, contract management, and your execution teams.

Detail every target mentioned in your strategy in terms of resources.

Lastly, time is a crucial factor. You can now play with scenarios and success ratios to determine the optimal timeline for achieving your goals. For example, you may be able to achieve your goals within two years, with a 90% success rate; or within three years with the same success rate. The financial controller/planner can help you determine how these scenarios will affect your business case.

Overall, setting yourself up for success without contractors requires a proactive approach to managing your resources and investments. It is crucial to ensure you have the right expertise and support in place, to help you make informed decisions and achieve your objectives. By incorporating a well-designed financial plan and approach into your execution strategy, you can position yourself for long-term success and achieve your goals without relying on outsiders.

Summary

To successfully actualize your digital strategy, you need to:

- Foster an innovation culture, starting with disruption. When a business is taken out of its comfort zone, people will innovate as they strive to regain their lost balance.

- Appoint a program lead who will work with the business lead to ensure a smooth handover from external consultants.

- Have a strong communication strategy to get all stakeholders aligned. This might involve improving your own communication skills.

- Convert your execution strategy into tangible financial outcomes and allocate resources accordingly. Note: If necessary, call in a financial expert to help you make good investment decisions.

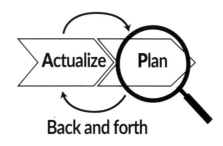

Back and forth

6
RAPID Phase 3:
Plan For Success

A well-crafted plan, supported by stakeholders, is crucial for success in any endeavor. However, it's essential to remember that a plan is never set in stone—it may require changes along the way. In this chapter we will delve into the five key pillars that contribute to an effective plan. These pillars are:

1. **Planning with the end in mind:** One of the essential aspects of planning is to determine the end goal first, and then work backward to create a roadmap that will help you achieve your objectives.

2. **Foolproof planning:** A successful plan is one that is carefully thought out, considering all possible obstacles and challenges that may arise. It is

crucial to prepare contingency plans to minimize the risks.

3. **Embedded monitoring:** It is essential to monitor the execution of the plan from the outset to ensure that it remains on track. This monitoring should include regular progress reviews and performance metrics.

4. **Priority effect:** A key aspect of planning is prioritizing tasks and activities and ensuring that the most critical and impactful tasks are completed first. The priority effect also encompasses the competition of other programs and projects within the company that may compete with your tasks.

5. **Visualization:** Visualizing the plan can be an effective tool for helping to make it a reality. Creating visual representations such as diagrams or flowcharts can help to clarify the steps required to achieve the desired outcome.

We will next explore these pillars in greater detail, peeling back the layers to reveal the key components of a successful plan.

Plan with the end in mind

In 2007 I was involved in the merger of two major banks, within the customer data and agreements area. We divided our approach in roughly two phases:

Phase 1: Get target ready
Phase 2: Migrate to target

During Phase 1 we worked on the business procuration functionality, which had to be ready in time and compatible with our customer channels, before migration—Phase 2—could happen.

In March of that year, a leading board member queried whether we could be ready in October, as the migration was planned for November. We said we couldn't and were called to the boardroom to explain. The chief operations officer expressed his concerns about reputational damage if we failed to deliver on time. After discussing the matter with my project lead and senior manager, I stated that October would be the soonest possible delivery date, even in the most optimistic scenario.

The COO then pulled an old management trick by stating that we would deliver in September along with the channels, and the migration would take place on the weekend of 6/7 November. Although I was taken aback, I felt excited and fired up to make it happen. We immediately went to work and planned backward from September the same goals and activities that we had thought would happen in October.

This meant additionally working outside office hours until the very end, and some team members dropped out due to the pressure. We then successfully implemented the project over two weekends in September, but the tension among the management to whom we reported was severe.

After the project, I felt a bit ashamed when I spoke to a colleague who had dropped out due to stress. However, he surprised me by saying that it had been the best project ever, because it brought everyone together to achieve one goal. As the end goal was in everyone's mind and we planned accordingly, it helped us to succeed.

HOW IT WORKS: Plan with the end in mind

A leading technology firm that specializes in developing innovative software solutions aimed to expand its market share in the healthcare sector by developing a state-of-the-art patient-management system.

Program objective

To create a comprehensive patient-management system that improves operational efficiency, enhances patient care, and enables seamless communication between healthcare providers, patients, and administrative staff.

Step 1: Determining the end goal

Before initiating the planning process, the management team conducted extensive market research and engaged in discussions with healthcare professionals to determine the desired outcomes.

The end goal was defined as: Develop a patient-management system that streamlines administrative tasks, improves patient engagement, and facilitates efficient communication between healthcare providers and patients.

Step 2: Identifying key objectives

The key objectives necessary to achieve the end goal were:

1. Streamline administrative tasks: Simplify and automate administrative processes such as patient registration, appointment scheduling, billing, and insurance-claim processing.
2. Enhance patient engagement: Develop features that empower patients to access their health records, schedule appointments online, receive appointment reminders, and communicate securely with healthcare providers.
3. Facilitate communication: Enable seamless communication between healthcare providers, patients, and administrative staff through secure messaging, telehealth capabilities, and real-time updates on appointment status and test results.

Step 3: Creating a roadmap

The planning team worked backward to create a roadmap in four phases outlining the necessary steps to achieve success.

Phase 1: Research and analysis

- Conduct in-depth market research to understand the specific needs and pain points of healthcare providers and patients.

- Analyze existing patient-management systems in the market to identify gaps and opportunities for improvement.
- Gather input from healthcare professionals, patients, and administrative staff through surveys and interviews.

Phase 2: System design and development

- Develop a comprehensive system architecture that encompasses all key features and functionalities.
- Prioritize user-friendly interfaces and intuitive navigation to ensure ease of use for healthcare providers and patients.
- Incorporate data security measures to protect patient information and comply with healthcare regulations.

Phase 3: Testing and refinement

- Conduct extensive testing to ensure the system functions smoothly, identifying and resolving any bugs and glitches.
- Seek feedback from healthcare providers, patients, and administrative staff to refine the system and enhance user experience.
- Conduct pilot testing, in collaboration with a select group of healthcare providers and patients, to validate the system's effectiveness.

Phase 4: Deployment and training

- Roll out the patient-management system across healthcare facilities, ensuring seamless integration with existing systems and workflows.
- Provide comprehensive training to healthcare providers and administrative staff to ensure they are proficient in using the system.

- Communicate with patients and educate them about the benefits and functionalities of the system, encouraging their active participation.

Step 4: Execution and evaluation

The company executed the roadmap according to the defined phases, continuously monitoring the progress and evaluating the results. The implementation team regularly assessed the system's performance against the established objectives, seeking feedback from stakeholders and making necessary adjustments to ensure the system aligned with the desired outcomes.

Conclusion

The clear definition of the end goal and the subsequent roadmap enabled the company to stay focused on achieving the desired outcomes, resulting in a comprehensive solution that met the needs of healthcare providers, patients, and administrative staff.

Foolproof planning

Effective planning involves more than only building in a buffer for potential setbacks—it is essential to identify risks and uncertainties from the outset and to create robust contingency plans to address them. This requires a thorough risk assessment process, ideally using expert panels to calculate the probability of each identified risk. These risks should then be incorporated into the project plan, with specific miti-gation measures clearly defined.

To ensure the project stays on track, Eliyahu M Goldratt's theory of constraints can be applied, along with team buffering to manage any setbacks.[16] This might involve identifying and securing backup infra-structure and technical support resources, defining communication protocols to address outages or other issues, and developing a plan to handle unexpected spikes in traffic.

It's also important to regularly review and update the plan to ensure that potential issues are identified and addressed in a timely manner. By taking a proactive approach to risk management and contingency plan-ning, you can maximize the chances of success and minimize any negative impact from unforeseen issues.

Embedded monitoring

When drafting the plan, you should incorporate met-rics from the start and get your director to sign them off. In this way, progress is transparent, and it is easy to forecast success and necessary deviations.

Key elements for a dashboard for this are:

---

16 EM Goldratt, *The Goal*

- **Clear and concise presentation.** The dashboard should provide a clear and easy-to-understand presentation of the metrics, using charts, graphs, or tables to effectively communicate progress.

- **Real-time or near real-time updates.** The dashboard should provide real-time or near real-time updates on the progress of the project or program, enabling the team to react quickly to any issues or deviations.

- **Customizable view.** The dashboard should allow each stakeholder to customize their view, according to their role and responsibilities, so they can focus on the metrics that are most relevant to them.

- **Historical data.** The dashboard should include historical data, allowing the team to track progress over time and identify trends.

- **Alerts and notifications.** The dashboard should be able to send alerts and notifications when a metric falls outside of the acceptable range, so that the team can take corrective action immediately.

- **Integration with other systems.** The dashboard should be able to integrate with other systems and tools such as project management software, to provide a comprehensive view of the project or program.

Priority effect

In the world of program and project management, it's essential to be aware of the *priority effect*—the fact that when multiple projects are vying for attention and resources, some will inevitably take priority over others.

This was a lesson we learned the hard way during an IT transformation program in 2015. At one point, the company was experiencing a spate of outages like many companies at that time. It was caused by DDOS (distributed denial of service) attacks, which led to failing infrastructure and applications—an easy way for hackers to cause trouble via low-budget attacks. In response, the board launched a resilience program led by one of the directors. As the director reported directly to the most senior board within the company, all his decisions and priorities were accepted. This had an immediate impact on our program—suddenly, we were no longer the top-priority program and engineers were focusing on the resilience program instead of our contracted work.

To mitigate the impact on progress, we shifted from a contract-led strategy to a hands-on approach. This allowed us to maintain momentum and keep making progress, despite the challenges we faced. Ultimately, we were successful in delivering the projects on time and to a high standard.

The key takeaways from this experience were as follows.

- Always be aware of the priority effect and understand that your project may be deprioritized at any time.

- Continuously look for any cascading effects that could impact your project, and be prepared to adapt quickly if necessary.

- Renegotiate your setup with your team and director as needed, and be prepared to shift your strategy in response to changing circumstances.

- Direct contact with a senior board member is the key to success. Often, when there is direct contact about progress with the most senior board member involved, or when a board member takes a leading role—as business lead, for example—the project is more likely to be successful.

Bearing these principles in mind will increase your chances of delivering a project that meets or exceeds expectations.

Visualization

As mentioned in previous chapters, visualization helps in the success of any project. A comprehensive and clear plan—depicting how different streams and activities align, according to themes—is crucial. This helps all stakeholders understand the big picture and collaborate effectively to achieve desired outcomes.

The following approaches and tools will help you.

- Agile tools like Kanban boards, storyboards, and backlog tools assist teams in managing tasks, tracking progress, and collaborating effectively. They are especially useful for Agile projects requiring frequent iteration and adjustments.

- Gantt charts are useful for visualizing the project timeline. Each task or activity is represented as a horizontal bar on the chart, making it easier for senior management to understand. Furthermore, funnel visualization can help all stakeholders understand where they are in the process.

- An Obeya room (virtual or physical) serves as a central hub for the project, where stakeholders, teams, and outsourcing parties can review progress and make decisions. To give these parties a better understanding of the context and make them more likely to support the outcome, you can lead them through the Obeya room and demonstrate the project's progress.

By incorporating visualization into the planning process and leveraging tools like these, project managers can create a cohesive, collaborative, and effective project plan that increases the chances of success. Numerous online tools such as Miro and Mural support this approach.

EXAMPLE: Obeya room

A large, well-established manufacturing company was looking to improve its digital capabilities. An Obeya initiative helped in aligning the company's various departments and teams around common goals.

The company first determined the strategic objectives it wanted to achieve with the digital transformation. These included improving efficiency, increasing innovation, and reducing costs. The company also identified several Key Performance Indicators (KPIs) it wanted to measure and improve such as lead times, product quality, and customer satisfaction.

Next, it identified the stakeholders and roles involved in the initiative, including executives, department managers, and team leads. A physical Obeya space, created in a central location, was accessible and visible to all stakeholders. The space was designed with visual aids such as charts, diagrams, and maps, which displayed the company's current digital capabilities, goals and plans, performance and progress, issues and solutions, and actions and responses.

To establish a rhythm for meetings and evaluations, the company set up regular meetings with stakeholders in the Obeya space to discuss the status of the initiative, share feedback and ideas, identify and solve problems, make decisions, and take actions.

The meetings were kept short and focused on results, using a standard agenda and format, which included items such as strategic direction, performance, value plan, difficult issues, and actions and responses.

Finally, the Obeya initiative was monitored and evaluated, tracking KPIs and outcomes, and comparing them with the company's goals and expectations. The tasked team analyzed root causes of any gaps or deviations and adjusted the company's goals, plans, and actions accordingly.

By implementing the Obeya initiative, the company was able to better align its departments and teams around common goals, and improve communication and collaboration across the organization. It also saw improvements in efficiency, innovation, and cost reduction, as well as gains in lead times, product quality, and customer satisfaction. Overall, the Obeya initiative helped the company stay competitive in the digital age and continue to thrive in the marketplace

---

In order to cover all necessary topics when planning your goals, I strongly recommend envisioning the steps necessary to reach your objective(s). A useful tool for visualizing this is the program funnel I have developed, which has been included as a reference for your future use. It starts with the Idea phase and follows the RAPID flow as well.

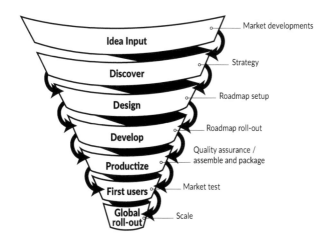

Visualization: Generic program funnel

To enhance your success planning, I encourage you to visualize the development process across three critical levels:

1. The strategy (or board) level with its pivotal value-adding moments—the ambitions

2. The ambition level, where middle management assumes accountability for delivering proof points that contribute to the strategy and overall value

3. The execution level, where engineering teams primarily produce increments, generating proof points for the middle layer

The presence of clear reports between these layers allows you to consistently monitor your progress towards achieving success.

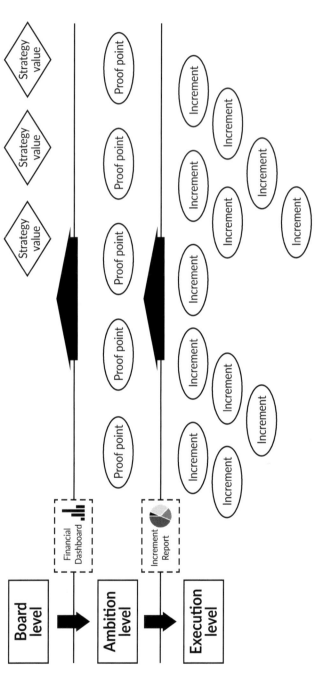

Visualization: example of program levels

Summary

Robust planning is essential for any project to succeed. A successful plan requires careful consideration of the five pillars:

1. Planning with the end in mind involves working backward to create a roadmap for achieving your objectives.

2. Foolproof planning requires considering all possible challenges and preparing contingency plans.

3. Embedded monitoring ensures that the plan remains on track, with regular progress reviews and performance metrics.

4. Priority effect considers not only the completion of critical tasks first but also the competition between tasks of other programs and projects.

5. Visualization helps clarify the steps needed to achieve the desired outcome. A tool such as Obeya supports understanding and the conversation required to reach goals.

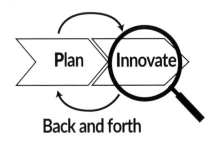

Plan | Innovate

Back and forth

7

RAPID Phase 4: Innovate Through Transformation

Ideas are never scarce because sources for idea inspiration are almost inexhaustible, but innovation realization is still the holy grail.

For years, across all sectors, around 70% of IT innovation changes have failed or seen unsatisfactory results. Governments across the globe have experienced the highest number of those unfortunate outcomes, while the financial sector has remained at the relatively favorable end of the scale. Between 2010 and 2020, successful projects across all sectors still do not constitute a third of the project portfolio.[17]

---

17 J Johnson, *CHAOS 2020: Beyond Infinity* (The Standish Group, 2021), https://standishgroup.myshopify.com, accessed October 13, 2023

With climate threats present, energy transformations at hand, and the advance of generative AI, now more than ever, we need to transform our habits. We need to find new ways of doing things to guarantee our wellbeing by achieving a higher project success rate.

In Chapter One I listed the most important developments in the field of technology in 2024. These developments will also drive solutions for our climate, energy transition, health, etc. For me important ones are:

- The breakthrough of quantum computing in the coming decade

- Data as an asset that provides access to prediction, and forms the basis for AI, policymaking, etc

- AI that will process data at a speed that is not humanly achievable, giving us insights we currently cannot imagine; for example, the use of AI in the treatment of breast cancer, which by far surpasses the expertise of individual scientists

- The development of the metaverse, which will offer us and our children new opportunities in education, such as reliving historical events, making learning a completely different experience, and driving new possibilities for logistics, for example where factories can be modeled to test their potential efficiency

- Creation of digital twins so that engineers do not have to be physically present to perform controls and repairs during dangerous work conditions (for example, at a nuclear reactor) but can operate remotely through their digital counterparts on-site

- Augmented reality in operating theaters, allowing every organ to be projected in 3D during surgery, increasing the precision of the operation and outcome

- Introduction of 6G, in combination with quantum computing, making hologram technology so real that you can be anywhere in the world and interact with real people or holograms at any other location, blurring the line between the physical and digital worlds

These transitions will come not only from multinationals but also—perhaps especially—from smaller businesses, where entrepreneurs want to convert their strategy into successful innovations, often with their own investments.

When the development momentum is there, you must be able to seize it, allowing you to be more successful than before. Use your intelligence, trust your instincts, and don't be afraid.

Let us now consider how to move from strategy into transformation and execution.

IT strategy

AI TRiSM ☐   ☐ Wi-Fi 6 and 7
Trust with Blockchain ☐   ☐ Sustainable technology
Applied observability ☐   ☐ Quantum computing
Internet of Things (IoT) ☐   ☐ Superapps
Cybersecurity ☐   ☐ Low-code development
Cloud computing ☐   ☐ AI and machine learning

Tick the boxes you want to invest in ☑

Example topics to consider for your innovation roadmap

Conscious choices for execution

The following questions need to be answered before commencing any transformation:

1. Why are we making this change, and how does it relate to our business strategy?

2. What is the expected result? How will we know if the change is successful?

3. How are we going to achieve the result?

4. With whom and with what resources are we going to achieve the result?

5. Where will the change take place?

6. When can we speak of successful moments?

7. Which iterations need to be completed when and against which criteria?

Personal qualities for successful execution in digital transformation are the same qualities you need for success in any project goal, and in life:

- **Eagerness.** Go for it; be motivated to the bone.

- **Discipline.** This is important to avoid falling into the pitfalls of the first point. Going for it is good, but if important fundamentals are overlooked— such as a clear framework on results, time, money, and resources—you're lost.

- **Control.** Be a player. Always play the ball or direct the game yourself, because that's how you determine the outcome of the game and therefore the result.

- **Simplicity.** Keep things simple.

- **Norm.** As the leader, you have to set the norm. Be tough on content and soft on relationships, but stick to the norm. It's not for nothing that Bruce W Tuckman developed a whole team-development theory—Forming, Storming, Norming, Performing (and Adjourning)—the stages every change team goes through.[18]

---

18 BW Tuckman, "Developmental sequence in small groups", *Psychological Bulletin*, 63 (1965), 384–399

- **Continuous communication.** Communication also includes listening, because then you have the eyes *and* ears of your team as additional support.

- **Good atmosphere.** During hard work, there may and even must be moments of relaxation, because that creates an even stronger bond for achieving results.

- **Creativity in spreading your message.** Creativity in spreading your transformation message is crucial. One effective method is to utilize subliminal messaging through your team's background. For example, you can have your transformation goals displayed behind you during discussions. This ensures that everyone you engage with, whether consciously or unconsciously, is left with a lasting impression of the objectives you aim to accomplish. Of course, if necessary, you can also explicitly highlight these goals during your interactions. There will be no ambiguity about the definition of success in this way.

Practical guidance

There are a number of useful principles that can be applied without having to implement a whole methodology, as outlined next.

Visual management

Visualize your plans, your prototype, and everything else that goes along with it. It's helpful to create a space (such as an Obeya room, as in Chapter Six) where people can come together to see the strategy translated into execution and results. In the same space, have a wall for operations so that connections between change and operation can be made. This immediately increases context awareness and collaboration. A planning space can also be created virtually with Miro, Mural, or other tools available on the market.

PDCA cycle

The PDCA cycle—or the Deming Cycle,[19] as it's commonly referred to—is part of the Lean management philosophy.[20] PDCA stands for:

- **Plan:** What is the plan? Use the seven questions of conscious execution mentioned earlier, as a framework for evaluation.

- **Do:** Start—execute your plan.

- **Check:** Check if you're meeting the predefined criteria.

---

19 K Feldman, *How PDCA Can Help Improve Organizational Efficiency*

20 AR Siddiqui, "Lean Philosophy: The Way Of Business That Gave Rise To Industry Giants", *Forbes* (14 January 2021), www.forbes.com/sites/theyec/2021/01/14/lean-philosophy-the-way-of-business-that-gave-rise-to-industry-giants, accessed September 18, 2023

- **Act:** If you do meet the criteria, initiate the next phase. If not, go back to the Check phase and repeat the cycle until the predefined successful outcome is achieved.

The kata principle[21]

Kata—a Japanese term also used in martial arts—refers to a focused way of mastering certain defense or attack techniques, depending on the goal you want to achieve. It is especially effective as an innovation driver.

You can easily understand the simple system of an improvement kata, which has four steps:

Step 1: Understand and establish the direction you want to go in.

Step 2: Understand the current state.

Step 3: Determine your experiment, with the desired state attached to it.

Step 4: Determine how you can iterate toward your goal state, for example, by using a PDCA cycle.

In addition, ensure progress through a weekly coaching moment, with the following simple questions:

---

21 M Rother, *TOYOTA KATA: A way to practice and develop scientific thinking in everyday work*, www-personal.umich.edu/~mrother/ Homepage.html, accessed September 18, 2023

1. Where do you want to be?

2. Where are you now?

3. What obstacles are standing in your way, and what are you working on now?

4. What is the next step, and what do you expect to achieve?

5. When can others come and see what you have learned from this step?

Consider the following when asking the questions above:

- What was your last step?

- What was your expectation?

- What really happened?

- What did you learn?

Finally, at each step in the kata process, the change team needs to:

- Document it

- Announce it

- Do it

- Check it

- If the result has been achieved, end it

HOW IT WORKS: The kata principle

The example given here is software version control in a microservice environment. In this scenario we applied the following tools: Visual management, the PDCA (Deming) cycle, and the kata principle.

Step 1: Understand and establish the direction you want to go in.

The development team and stakeholders come together to agree on the desired improvements in software version control for the microservice environment. They establish the goal of achieving more efficient and reliable version control processes. To visually represent this goal, they opt for the Kanban board as their visual management and progress tool.

Step 2: Understand the current state.

The team assesses the current state of software version control in the microservice environment. They analyze the existing version control practices; identify any bottlenecks, inconsistencies, or issues; and gather relevant data. To visualize the current state, they update the Kanban board with information about the current workflows, bottlenecks, and pain points.

Step 3: Determine your experiment, with the desired state attached to it.

According to the analysis of the current state, the team decides on an experiment to address the identified issues. For example, they may choose to implement a more streamlined branching strategy, or adopt a new version control tool specifically designed for microservices. They add the details of this experiment, including the desired state, to the Kanban board as a visual representation of the planned improvement.

Step 4: Determine how you can iterate toward your goal state, for example, using a PDCA cycle.

The team plans the implementation of the chosen experiment in iterations. They break the implementation down into smaller steps and define measurable milestones to track progress. They decide to use the PDCA (Deming) cycle to guide their iterative approach. To visualize the iterations and progress, they create swim lanes or columns on the Kanban board representing each step of the PDCA cycle. They then move the corresponding tasks or cards across the board as they progress.

During regular coaching moments, the team addresses the following questions to ensure progress:

1. Where do you want to be?

The team discusses the desired state they are aiming to achieve in terms of improved software version control. They update the Kanban board with visual indicators or symbols, representing the desired state.

2. Where are you now?

The team provides an update on current progress, highlighting any challenges or successes. They visually represent the current state on the Kanban board, reflecting the movement of tasks or cards within the swim lanes or columns.

3. What obstacle(s) are standing in your way, and what are you working on now?

The team identifies any obstacles hindering their progress and shares the steps they are currently taking to overcome them. They add visual indicators or markers on the Kanban board to represent the obstacles and the actions being taken to address them.

4. What is the next step, and what do you expect to achieve?

The team outlines the next action they will take to move closer to the desired state and states their expected outcomes. They update the Kanban board by moving tasks or cards to the next step or swim lane, visually indicating the progression.

5. When can others come and see what you have learned from this step?

The team schedules regular checkpoints to demonstrate the progress made and share the lessons learned. They set up review sessions, where the Kanban board serves as a visual reference to showcase the progress and insights gained.

Reflection questions

After completing each step, the team uses these questions to reflect on their progress, updating the Kanban board or equivalent with visual indicators or annotations after each one:

- **What was your last step?**

  The team describes the actions taken during the previous step to improve software version control.

- **What was your expectation?**

  The team articulates their anticipated outcomes or improvements from the last step. They compare the expected outcomes with the actual results.

- **What really happened?**

  The team shares the actual results and outcomes achieved during the last step.

- **What did you learn?**

  The team reflects on the lessons learned from the last step, identifying successes, challenges, and areas for further improvement.

Change-team actions

At each step, the change team follows these actions, updating the Kanban board or equivalent as above:

- **Document it:** The team documents the changes made, including the specific improvements implemented in software version control.

- **Announce it:** The team communicates the changes and improvements to relevant stakeholders, ensuring that everyone is aware of the updates. They add a designated section for stakeholder communication to the Kanban board or equivalent.

- **Do it:** The team implements the planned changes, following the established experiment and iteration process.

- **Check it:** The team evaluates the results of the implemented changes, comparing them against the expected outcomes and goals. They update the Kanban board with visual indicators or metrics that reflect the evaluation results.

- **If the result has been achieved, end it:** If the desired results are achieved and the software version control has improved as intended, the team considers the step complete. They visually mark the completion of the step on the Kanban board and move on to the next improvement iteration.

By incorporating visual management, along with the PDCA cycle and the kata principle way of working, through a Kanban board or similar tool, the team can have a clear, shared understanding of the improvement goals; track progress visually; identify obstacles; reflect on learnings; and communicate the changes effectively. This visual representation enhances transparency, collaboration, and the overall success of improving software version control in a microservice environment.

Theory of constraints

Here we apply Eliyahu M Goldratt's method to innovation.[22]

- Determine the iterations necessary to achieve the result.

- Determine the required investment budget for each iteration.

- Identify the critical path for each iteration.

Repeat the following steps until the result is achieved.

---

22   EM Goldratt, *The Goal*

1. Identify the limiting factor.

2. Examine the process in which the limiting factor occurs, and ensure there is no waste in that process.

3. Ensure all processes are subordinated to the limiting process and that the identified limiting factor is used optimally.

4. Determine whether the limiting factor can be solved by expanding capacity.

5. Once the limiting factor is resolved, look for the next limiting factor and start again at step 1.

Student syndrome

This term refers metaphorically to a typical student, who starts revising the night before an exam. You might well have team members like this.

If you have a team that needs to perform tasks to achieve a result, you will of course have planned those tasks in consultation with the team. Next, sit down again with your team to squeeze all the nonessential time out of the planning. Then schedule the squeezed-out time—the slack—at the end. Agree with the team that, if they need some slack, they can always arrange that with you in the weekly team meeting so that everyone understands why some slack was needed.

This results in several things:

- People become more aware of time pressures and requirements.

- You get a learning effect according to factual situations.

- With experience, you can anticipate when the slack will be needed. Eventually, it won't be needed at all because you will have included it in your planning.

Design sprint

A design sprint is a collaborative process that allows you to quickly test and validate ideas by combining expertise from different fields. By bringing together a team of experts for a short period, such as a week, you can experiment with different iterations. Before investing significant time and resources into development, you will learn which iteration will produce the desired results. This process helps you to rapidly prototype and test ideas, following steps on five consecutive days:

1. Understand and define

2. Ideate

3. Decide and prototype

4. Test

5. Iterate and plan

EXAMPLE: Design sprint

Let's say a company conducts a design sprint to develop a new mobile application to enhance their customer experience.

Day 1: Understand and define

The team—consisting of designers, developers, marketers, and other relevant stakeholders—come together to understand the project goals, user needs, and challenges. They define a clear problem statement and set specific objectives for the design sprint.

Day 2: Ideate

An ideas-storming session generates a wide range of ideas to solve the defined problem. Techniques such as mind mapping, sketching, and rapid idea generation are used to explore possibilities. The team leverages their diverse expertise to come up with innovative concepts for the mobile application.

Day 3: Decide and prototype

The team evaluates and selects the most promising concepts to prototype. They make decisions about the features, user interface, and overall design of the application. With the help of designers and UX specialists, they create a low-fidelity prototype that represents the key functionalities and interactions of the app.

Day 4: Test

The team conducts user-testing sessions to gather feedback on the prototype. They recruit a small group of target users and observe their interactions with the prototype. The team members take notes, record insights, and according to user feedback, identify areas that need improvement. This user testing helps validate assumptions and identify potential issues early in the process.

Day 5: Iterate and plan

According to the feedback received, the team iterates on the prototype, making necessary adjustments and improvements. They refine the design, address user concerns, and fine-tune the functionality. Additionally, they plan the next steps, deciding on the features to prioritize on the development roadmap.

By the end of the design sprint week, the team has gained valuable insights and feedback from users, allowing them to make informed decisions about the mobile application's design and functionality. The rapid prototyping and testing approach has saved time and resources that would have been spent on developing an application without user validation. The team can now move forward with confidence, armed with a solid understanding of user needs and a validated concept for the mobile application.

Which methodology?

Until the early 2010s, most multinationals and governments used Waterfall methodology.[23] This relied

---

23   WW Royce, "Managing the Development of Large Software Systems", *Technical Papers of Western Electronic Show and Convention*, 26 (1970)

on rigid phases, lengthy preliminary studies, and formal change procedures, resulting in long lead times and products that were often outdated by the time of launch.

The introduction of Agile (a project management style) and Scrum (a method used to implement Agile) marked a cultural revolution, empowering executing teams with greater autonomy. It led to the expansion of the Agile Manifesto[24] and the introduction of methods like Scaled Agile Framework (SAFe); the Large-Scale Scrum (LESS) framework; and the Spotify model, which organizes around tasks rather than following specific principles.[25] However, conflicts between these methods sometimes led to confusion in the workplace.

Many people in the change industry promote the Agile Scrum methodology, largely because it adheres to the mantra of *fail fast, learn fast* and because it allows for fast and easy deployment of minimum viable products. It is geared toward beating the competition to enter the market quickly with minimal losses. It also allows the proposed strategy to be tested early on to see if it works in practice. The feedback loop is as short as possible. However, it's important to acknowledge

---

24 Agile Alliance, "What is the Agile Manifesto?", www.agilealliance. org/agile101/the-agile-manifesto, accessed September 18, 2023

25 L Quick, "SAFe vs Agile frameworks: Scrum Scale vs LeSS vs Spotify", knowledgehut blog (September 5 2023), www.knowledgehut.com/blog/ agile/safe-vs-scrum-scale-vs-less-vs-spotify, accessed September 18, 2023

that the speed of each market can vary, so some degree of relativity is necessary in this context.

If you are not familiar with Agile Scrum or similar methodology, you can rest assured that, as long as your changes are managed by a small team (somewhere between five and fifty people), a good mentality with some basic change-initiative principles is sufficient. It is not always necessary to work to the letter of a methodology.

It's vital to set clear guidelines on results before implementing any methodology. To determine the guidelines for your project, answer the questions listed earlier:

- Why are we making this change, and how does it relate to our business strategy?

- What is the expected result? How will we know if the change is successful?

- How are we going to achieve the result?

- With whom and with what resources are we going to achieve the result?

- Where will the change take place?

- When can we speak of successful moments?

- Which iterations need to be completed when and against which criteria?

Agile and Scrum (called Agile Scrum when used together) are flexible and allow for continuous feedback and adjustments. One common mistake is failing to define the Agile Scrum team's goal in the broader context of the organization. Naming the team is not as important as describing the fundamental value it brings, which should be clearly defined to ensure that the team can disband itself when it has achieved its objective or if the team proves to be redundant.

It's worth noting that Agile Scrum may not be the best fit for every project. "Small Projects" with a defined end in mind is needed as an alternative project management framework, following aspects of Waterfall methodology but in an agile way, providing a more structured approach. For example, data center migrations with well-defined outcomes may benefit from a more structured approach. In such cases, you can keep your teams in place and use traditional project management techniques. However, clear communication is essential to ensure that teams understand why this approach is necessary.

Establishing an effective team setup is crucial for successful project management. BusDevOps, DevOps, and DevSecOps methodologies aim to foster collaboration and streamline processes between business, development, and IT operations teams. BusDevOps supports bridging the historically typical gap between business and IT, by forming collective teams across the domains. DevOps emphasizes communication, collaboration, and automation, while DevSecOps adds a security layer to the process.

Kanban is an alternative project management methodology that can be used in place of Scrum. Kanban focuses on visualizing workflow and limiting work in progress, while Scrum emphasizes self-organizing teams and time-boxed iterations.

Additionally, the Team Topology framework can improve team performance by defining optimal team structures and communication patterns. This framework recommends four types of team setups: Stream-aligned teams, Enabling teams, Complicated subsystem teams, and Platform teams.

By carefully defining team setups, selecting the right methodology, and following a framework such as Team Topology or Agile, project managers increase their chances of successfully executing their projects.

Dashboards for board-level comfort

It's more important than ever for board members to be able to quickly assess their company's performance and identify areas for improvement. Dashboards offer an excellent way to do just that, by providing a visual representation of critical data in an easily understandable format. By presenting data in real time, dashboards help board members stay up to date on key metrics such as sales, customer retention, and market share. With this information readily available, board members can make timely and informed decisions that drive the company toward success.

At the same time, finance is an essential function in any organization, and board members must therefore have a clear understanding of the financial implications of their decisions. Financial data such as revenue, expenses, and profit margins can help board members evaluate the success of past initiatives and inform future strategic planning. By using predictive analytics and machine learning, finance can become even more attractive for first movers—pioneering products or services in the market—in the IT landscape. Predictive analytics can help board members identify trends and patterns in financial data that may not be apparent at first glance. Machine learning can enable the organization to make more accurate financial predictions, ensuring that board members have the information they need to make informed decisions.

By becoming familiar with dashboards and finance, and using innovative technologies and data-driven decision-making, board members can help steer their organization toward success. Ultimately, this approach can help the organization gain a competitive advantage and become a first mover in their industry, setting the stage for future growth.

*Example of an automated financial
dashboard, with dummy data[26]*

---

26   Financial Dashboard by permission of Madiha Mouchtak

Predictive analytics

Setting up a project resulting in predictive analytics involves several key steps:

1. **Define the problem.** The first step in setting up a project resulting in predictive analytics is to clearly define the problem you want to solve. This could be anything from predicting customer behavior to forecasting sales figures.

2. **Gather and prepare data.** Once you've defined the problem, you need to gather the relevant data. This could include historical data, customer demographics, and other relevant information. It's important to ensure that the data is accurate, complete, and relevant to the problem at hand.

3. **Explore the data:** Before you start building a predictive model, it's important to explore the data and look for patterns and relationships. This can be done using data visualization tools and techniques such as correlation analysis.

4. **Select a predictive model.** Once you've explored the data, you need to select an appropriate predictive model. This could include regression analysis, decision trees, neural networks, or other techniques depending on the problem you're trying to solve.

5. **Train the model.** After selecting a predictive model, you need to train it using the historical data you've gathered. This involves using algorithms and statistical techniques to find the best model parameters and build an accurate model.

6. **Test the model.** Once you've trained the model, you need to test it using a separate set of data. This helps ensure that the model is accurate and can generalize well to new data.

7. **Deploy the model.** Finally, you need to deploy the model in a production environment, where it can be used to make predictions and informed decision-making. This could involve integrating the model with existing systems and processes and ensuring that it's maintained and updated as needed.

Overall, this requires a combination of technical expertise, domain knowledge, and analytical skills. It's important to have a clear understanding of the problem you're trying to solve, as well as the data and techniques needed to build an accurate and effective predictive model.

Summary

This chapter has laid out the clear stages in your choice of approach to achieve successful project execution:

1. To move from IT strategy to execution, you first need to answer the seven questions at the start of this chapter. If the execution team or director is not able to answer these questions then it will never become a success. These questions are therefore the basics for the definition of success.

2. Define your team's project methodology, such as Scrum, Kanban, or Project Drive, based on your project's goals. Then choose the best practices described in this chapter, such as visual management, TOC, kata, etc. Once you've made these decisions, ensure that all team members understand and are committed to them.

3. In addition to the team setup, board-level comfort with a dashboard is essential. This will enable you to communicate your strategy and progress regularly to the board, showing them how your innovation will create value and drive business growth. Embedding predictive analytics in reports for board members is a great way to demonstrate the potential of your innovation.

Answer all the execution questions in advance to avoid mistakes and save time in the long run. It's also essential to create a winner mentality within your team by fostering a culture of innovation, trust, and collaboration.

While using proven tips from methodologies, don't be dogmatic about implementing entire methods. Instead, tailor the approach to your specific needs and context.

Feedback from a mentor, outsider, or coach can also be beneficial for improving your innovation strategy and building a strong team culture.

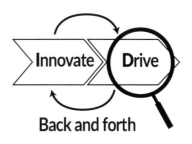

Innovate Drive

Back and forth

8
RAPID Phase 5:
Drive Growth

How do you move from carrying out your digital transformation to driving the strategy forward securely? Operating in a digital environment has become a necessity for individuals, businesses, and organizations of all sizes. Digital platforms have become the primary means of communication, networking, marketing, and conducting business transactions.

Moving to a digital environment requires a shift in mindset and approach, along with the different set of skills and tools. To be successful in this environment, it is crucial to have a strong understanding of digital technology and how it can be leveraged to achieve your goals.

One of the main advantages of operating in a digital environment is the ability to reach a global audience. Digital platforms offer businesses and individuals the opportunity to connect with customers, partners, and collaborators from all over the world, breaking down geographical barriers and enabling new opportunities for growth and expansion. However, operating in a digital environment also poses unique challenges such as the need for cybersecurity and privacy protection, as well as the importance of creating and maintaining a strong online reputation. It is essential to be mindful of these challenges and take proactive steps to mitigate them.

Overall, operating in a digital environment requires adaptability, creativity, and a willingness to learn and embrace new technologies. Those who can effectively navigate this landscape can gain a significant competitive advantage and position themselves for success in the digital age.

Operations in a digital environment

Businesses and organizations must navigate a unique set of challenges and risks to be successful in a digital environment. Let's consider the main ones.

Cybersecurity risks

This is one of the most significant risks. The potential for data breaches, hacking, and other cyber threats has become a prevalent concern. Businesses must implement measures to protect sensitive data and prevent cyberattacks.

To effectively navigate the risk of cybersecurity breaches in a digital environment, businesses and organizations must take several steps.

1. Conduct a comprehensive risk assessment to identify potential vulnerabilities and areas of weakness in a digital infrastructure. This assessment should include an evaluation of existing security measures such as firewalls, antivirus software, and encryption protocols.

2. Implement robust cybersecurity protocols that reflect best practice and comply with relevant regulations and industry standards which prevent data loss in the event of a cyberattack. This includes regular software updates and patches, multifactor authentication, and regular data backups.

3. Invest in employee training and awareness programs to ensure that all staff members are aware of the risks and how to mitigate them. This includes training on safe email, internet use and password management, and how to recognize and respond to potential threats such as phishing scams.

4. Consider outsourcing cybersecurity needs to a trusted third-party provider. This can be

especially beneficial for small and medium-sized businesses that may not have the resources or expertise to manage their own cybersecurity effectively. By working with a reputable provider, businesses can benefit from the latest technology and expertise in cybersecurity, while freeing up internal resources to focus on core business operations.

By taking these steps, businesses can protect sensitive data, prevent cyberattacks, and position themselves for success in the digital age.

Financial risks

Digital platforms offer numerous opportunities for businesses to streamline financial operations such as online payment systems and digital invoicing. However, with the rise of digital financial systems, new risks such as online fraud and identity theft have emerged. It is crucial to implement robust financial controls and secure payment systems to ensure that financial transactions are carried out safely and efficiently.

To effectively manage finance in a digital environment, businesses must implement several key measures.

1. Establish robust financial controls to prevent fraud and ensure the accuracy of financial records. This includes implementing secure access controls, regularly reconciling accounts, and implementing a system of checks and

balances to ensure that financial transactions are properly authorized and recorded.

2. Implement secure payment systems that comply with relevant regulations and industry standards. This includes using encryption and tokenization to protect sensitive data, implementing multifactor authentication for high-risk transactions, and monitoring transactions for signs of suspicious activity.

3. Invest in fraud detection and prevention tools that leverage AI and machine learning to identify and respond to potential threats. These tools can help businesses detect fraudulent activity in real time, minimize losses, and protect customer data.

4. Prioritize employee training and awareness programs to ensure that all staff members are aware of the risks and how to mitigate them. This includes training on safe financial practices (phishing scams again) and how to handle sensitive financial information.

By taking these steps, businesses can ensure that financial transactions are carried out safely and efficiently, and protect sensitive financial data.

Metrics

Digital platforms offer vast amounts of data that can be used to monitor and evaluate performance, customer behavior, and market trends. However, with the amount of data available, it can be challenging to identify meaningful insights and develop actionable strategies. To help with this, businesses should invest in data analytics tools and expertise to effectively interpret and leverage digital metrics.

To effectively leverage metrics in a digital environment, businesses must take several key steps.

1. Identify the specific metrics that are most relevant to their business objectives and align with their KPIs. This involves selecting metrics that provide insight into customer behavior, marketing performance, and operational efficiency.

2. Invest in data analytics tools and expertise to effectively interpret and make sense of the vast amounts of data available. This includes leveraging data visualization tools to present information in a meaningful and actionable way, using AI and machine-learning algorithms to identify patterns and trends, and engaging data scientists or analysts to help with the analysis.

3. Ensure that the data used to derive insights is of high quality and relevant. This involves implementing data-governance policies and procedures such as data cleansing and data validation, and regularly monitoring and auditing the data to ensure that it remains accurate and up to date.

4. Use the insights gained from digital metrics to develop actionable strategies and make data-driven decisions. This includes using the data to identify areas of opportunity and improvement, optimizing marketing campaigns, and enhancing the customer experience.

In this way businesses can stay ahead of the competition, adapt to changing market conditions, and drive growth and success in the digital age.

Business communication

Digital platforms offer numerous opportunities for businesses to connect with customers, partners, and stakeholders. However, with the increasing reliance on digital communication, it can be easy to lose the personal touch that comes with face-to-face interactions.

To achieve strong communication, businesses need to do the following.

1. Establish clear communication policies that prioritize clear and concise messaging, personalization, and engagement. This involves identifying the channels that are most effective for reaching different audiences, developing messaging guidelines that ensure consistency across channels, and engaging with customers and stakeholders through personalized and relevant content.

2. Invest in the digital communication tools and platforms that can help them reach their target audience. This includes email marketing tools, social media platforms, instant messaging apps, and video conferencing tools, among others. By leveraging the right tools, businesses can communicate with their customers and stakeholders more effectively and efficiently. At the time of writing, generative AI combined with chatbots is something that is worth considering, together with all the related pros and cons.

3. Maintain a human touch in digital communications. Businesses should use a conversational tone, with personalization and segmentation, and ensure that the customer's voice is heard. In this way they can build stronger relationships with customers and stakeholders, and foster trust and loyalty.

4. Regularly evaluate their communication strategies (for example, examining the impact of generative AI like ChatGPT, Bard, etc) to ensure that they are effective and resonating with their target audience. This involves tracking and analyzing metrics such as open rates, click-through rates, and engagement rates, and adjusting as needed.

By doing all this, businesses can build stronger relationships with their customers and stakeholders and succeed in the digital age.

Calamities

Mitigating the impact of calamities is another critical aspect of operating in a digital environment. You must be prepared for unexpected events such as natural disasters, cyberattacks, and global pandemics. Robust contingency plans and disaster recovery measures will ensure that you can continue to operate and serve customers in the face of unexpected disruptions.

To effectively mitigate the impact of calamities in a digital environment, businesses must adopt several key strategies.

1. Identify potential risks and threats and develop a comprehensive contingency plan that outlines how they will respond to each situation. This involves developing a crisis management team, establishing clear communication protocols, and outlining the specific steps the business will take in the event of a calamity.

2. Implement robust disaster recovery measures that ensure that critical systems and data are protected and can be restored in the event of an unexpected disruption. This involves implementing backup and recovery systems, establishing data protection policies, and regularly testing and updating disaster recovery plans.

3. Train employees on how to respond effectively to calamities. This includes conducting regular drills and simulations, providing training on

crisis communication and decision-making, and ensuring that employees understand their roles and responsibilities during a crisis.

4. Regularly evaluate and update contingency plans and disaster recovery measures to ensure that these remain effective and up to date. This involves conducting regular risk assessments, identifying areas for improvement, and making changes as needed.

In this way, businesses can ensure that they are prepared to respond to unexpected disruptions and continue to operate and serve their customers in the face of adversity.

In conclusion, operating in a digital environment requires businesses and organizations to navigate a complex landscape of risks and opportunities. Cybersecurity, finance, metrics, communication, and calamity mitigation are all critical components. By prioritizing these areas and investing in the necessary tools and expertise, businesses position themselves for success in the digital age.

Reality check on outsourcing

Outsourcing can be a valuable strategy for businesses, but it's important to be aware of its potential pitfalls, and to manage it effectively to maximize its benefits. One way to achieve this is to consider outsourcing as a service that needs to be managed just like any other business function. This means setting clear expectations and requirements, regularly monitoring and evaluating performance, and establishing effective communication channels with the outsourcing partner.

It's also important to carefully consider which aspects of the business to outsource and weigh up the benefits and risks of outsourcing specific functions such as labor, IT support, or customer service. Another strategy is to adopt a follow-the-sun approach—outsourcing to providers in different time zones can ensure that business operations are supported around the clock. By taking these steps, businesses can access specialized expertise, increase flexibility, and reduce costs.

When outsourcing services such as IT, there is a risk of losing control over the infrastructure and data that are vital to the organization. It is important to carefully evaluate the outsourcing provider's security and data protection measures, and to establish clear contractual agreements that address these concerns.

Another potential pitfall of outsourcing is the risk of hidden costs. While outsourcing can provide cost savings, it is important to carefully consider all the associated costs such as contract negotiations, management fees, and travel expenses.

Finally, it's important to be aware of the cultural differences that can arise when outsourcing to other countries, and to proactively address these through training and effective communication.

By approaching outsourcing with a clear strategy and learning from experiences, businesses can successfully navigate the potential pitfalls and reap the rewards that outsourcing can offer.

SRE standards

Site reliability engineering (SRE) practices have gained significant traction in recent years, particularly within tech companies that require high levels of system uptime and reliability.[27]

SRE practices aim to improve system reliability by bridging the gap between development and operations teams, and by setting shared goals and standards for service reliability. This approach recognizes that reliability is not only the responsibility of the operations team but also requires collaboration from all stakeholders, including developers, product managers, and customer support teams.

---

27 IBM, *What is site reliability engineering (SRE)?*, www.ibm.com/topics/site-reliability-engineering, accessed September 18, 2023

One of the core principles of SRE is the automation of repetitive, manual tasks that are prone to human error. This includes tasks such as configuration management, deployment, and testing. By automating these tasks, SRE teams can ensure that they are carried out consistently and with a high degree of accuracy, reducing the risk of system downtime and associated costs.

Another essential aspect of SRE is the use of monitoring and measurement to track system performance and proactively identify potential issues. SRE teams establish service level objectives (SLOs) and service level indicators (SLIs) to measure and track system performance against business objectives. SLOs define the desired level of service reliability that the system should achieve, while SLIs provide the metrics used to track system performance against those objectives.

In addition to SLOs and SLIs, SRE teams prioritize monitoring and alerting, to quickly identify and resolve system issues. This involves the use of automated tools and processes to collect data, and to trigger alerts when system performance falls outside of acceptable thresholds. By responding to these alerts quickly, SRE teams can minimize the impact of system issues and prevent them from escalating into more significant problems.

Another critical aspect of SRE is the emphasis on post-incident reviews to identify the root causes of system issues and develop strategies to prevent them from recurring. These reviews involve a detailed analysis of system performance data, incident logs, and stakeholder feedback, to identify the underlying causes of system issues. By sharing these insights with other teams, SRE teams can help to create a culture of continuous improvement and prevent similar issues from occurring in the future.

SRE practices also prioritize the establishment of clear communication channels and feedback mechanisms between various teams and between teams and stakeholders. This includes regular meetings and reporting on system performance, as well as the creation of formal escalation paths for issues that require urgent attention. By fostering clear communication channels, SRE teams can ensure that all stakeholders are aware of system issues and can work together effectively to resolve them.

Overall, SRE practices offer numerous benefits for businesses, including improved system reliability, reduced downtime, and improved customer satisfaction. By automating repetitive tasks, establishing clear SLOs and SLIs, prioritizing monitoring and alerting, conducting post-incident reviews, and fostering clear communication channels, SRE teams can help businesses to achieve a more efficient and reliable system.

Risk management is a crucial aspect of SRE practices. As with any technological implementation, there is always an inherent risk of failure or downtime. SRE teams aim to mitigate this risk by proactively identifying potential issues and implementing measures to prevent incidents or minimize their impact. This approach is based on the principles of risk management, which involves identifying potential risks, assessing their likelihood and impact, and implementing measures to mitigate or manage those risks.

SRE teams use a variety of tools and methodologies to manage risk, including incident management, change management, and disaster recovery planning. These practices help to ensure that the infrastructure and applications are highly available, scalable, and reliable. Additionally, SRE teams often work closely with other teams within the organization such as security and compliance teams to identify and mitigate potential security risks. By proactively managing risks and incidents, SRE teams can improve the overall reliability and resilience of the organization's IT infrastructure.

EXAMPLE: From the life of an ITIL (Information Technology Infrastructure Library) change manager

One day, the company's system went down for several hours, causing significant disruption to business operations, while also frustrating customers.

After conducting a post-incident review, the IT team discovered that the root cause of the issue was a misconfigured server setting that had been missed by the monitoring tools.

The team realized that they had been relying too heavily on manual processes to manage system configurations, and that they needed to implement more automated processes to reduce the risk of human error. They also recognized that clearer communication channels between development and operations teams were needed to ensure that everyone was aware of system changes and their potential impact.

By implementing these changes, the business was able to improve system reliability and prevent similar issues from occurring in the future.

Early in my career, I also worked as an ITIL change manager, with my primary focus on improving the operations process. One of my initiatives was to introduce checklists before changes could go live. The checklists helped us ensure that all necessary steps were followed and that we could catch potential issues before they impacted our systems. However, as fate would have it, I later became a program manager, where I found myself fighting against the very checklists I had created to achieve results quickly. This experience taught me several valuable lessons:

- I learned the importance of securing changes and mitigating risks when implementing new processes or systems.

- I realized that people's interpretation of rules can differ, depending on their perspective, which can cause friction in implementing new processes.

- I learned about the "oil stain effect"—the tendency for well-intentioned process improvements to eventually result in multiple toll gates and excessive bureaucracy.

These lessons have stayed with me throughout my career and have helped me to navigate the complex world of IT operations and project management. I've learned to strike a balance between necessary steps to mitigate risk and the impact on project timelines and the overall user experience.

Use AI and predictive analytics

To stay ahead of potential issues and minimize downtime, it's important to implement a robust monitoring system that utilizes AI and predictive analytics. By analyzing vast amounts of data in real time, AI-powered monitoring tools can detect anomalies and patterns that may not be immediately apparent to human operators. Predictive analytics can then be used to forecast potential issues before they arise, allowing organizations to take proactive steps to prevent them. In addition, AI and predictive analytics can be used to identify areas of improvement and optimize operations, helping businesses to reduce costs and improve efficiency.

To fully realize the benefits of AI and predictive analytics, it's important to invest in high-quality data infrastructure and ensure that your team is trained to effectively utilize these tools. It's also important to strike a balance between automation and human oversight, as the best results are often achieved through a combination of both. By implementing an effective monitoring system powered by AI and predictive analytics, organizations can gain a significant competitive advantage in the digital landscape.

By approaching these challenges with a proactive and informed mindset, businesses and individuals can position themselves for success in the digital age. To stay ahead of the competition, it is important to continuously adapt and evolve to the ever-changing digital landscape. Digital transformation is not a one-time event but rather a continuous process that requires constant learning, evaluation, and adjustment.

Summary

This chapter has covered the fundamental aspects of how digital transformation can drive growth, and the main risks and mitigation factors involved.

- It is important to have a strong understanding of digital technology and how it can be leveraged to achieve goals, especially considering the unique challenges that arise in the digital age.

- Cybersecurity and privacy protection, as well as maintaining a strong online reputation, are critical in maintaining a successful digital presence.

- Proactive management of financial risks, metrics, communication, and potential calamities is vital to remain safe and successful in the digital environment.

- Outsourcing can provide numerous advantages such as cost savings, access to specialized expertise, and increased flexibility. However, one of the biggest challenges of outsourcing is the potential loss of control over critical business functions.

- SRE practices can help businesses reduce downtime, improve system reliability, and increase efficiency. However, it is important to balance risk management and agility.

- Monitoring operations by using AI and predictive analytics can provide valuable insights into system performance and enable businesses to proactively identify and address issues.

PART THREE

YOUR JOURNEY STARTS HERE

Fulfillment can only be found by continuously
living up to your potential.

9

Navigating Potential Challenges To Digital Success

Businesses and organizations often face objections and concerns from stakeholders regarding digital transformation. These objections, ranging from apprehension about data privacy and security to fears of relinquishing control, can pose significant obstacles to achieving digital transformation goals.

By proactively addressing such concerns and offering viable solutions, it is possible to overcome objections and successfully navigate the path to digital success. This chapter will delve into some of the most common objections to digital transformation and provide practical strategies for addressing them. I will also dive deep into some of the typical concerns of CIOs.

Loss of control

Addressing concerns about loss of control is critical for any organization considering new software development methodologies. I will focus here on Agile DevOps and its variances, which in my opinion provide the smoothest journey toward and the best results from digital transformation, thanks to the combination of Agile practices with the DevOps culture of learning, growth, and improvement. As Agile DevOps has been implemented by most companies executing digital transformation, I will detail the main challenges here and how to overcome them.

The Agile DevOps methodology offers many advantages, including faster time-to-market processes, improved collaboration, and increased productivity. However, it is important to anticipate potential concerns from stakeholders and to consider how these can be overcome. The table outlines the most common concerns and mitigation measures.

Addressing concerns around control

Concern	Further detail	Mitigation
Losing control over critical business functions	Concerns around data security, regulatory compliance, and quality control	Emphasize the benefits of Agile DevOps, including increased transparency, improved risk management, and greater agility. Establish clear guidelines and communication channels, which can help address concerns about loss of control and ensure all stakeholders are on the same page.
Cost-cutting leading to reduced quality of services	Emphasis on efficiency leading to a lack of flexibility and innovation, if streamlining existing processes is prioritized over exploring new ideas	Strike a balance between service costs and efficiency, while maintaining a focus on quality and innovation.
	Negative impact on customer satisfaction, which could ultimately harm the business	Focus on service costs versus efficiency, to help the business maintain control over its budgets and ensure it is getting the best value for its investment.
Concerns about privacy and ethics due to the use of Big Data	While the use of Big Data can provide valuable insights and improve efficiency, it may also come at a cost to individual privacy and raise ethical concerns about the use of personal data	Be mindful of these concerns and take proactive steps to ensure that their use of Big Data is ethical and responsible.

EXAMPLE: Big data disaster

A leading technology company, which embraced the potential of Big Data to revolutionize their business, developed an advanced algorithm that could predict consumer behavior with remarkable accuracy.

They launched a targeted advertising campaign using this algorithm, but this had unintended consequences. People began to feel overwhelmed by invasive, personalized ads that seemed to follow them wherever they went. Privacy concerns arose as individuals realized their personal lives were being commodified for profit.

As dissatisfaction grew, the once loyal customers started to abandon the company. The ethical implications became a topic of public debate. The company's reputation took a significant hit, resulting in a severe backlash. It became clear that the unchecked use of Big Data had negatively impacted social values and eroded public trust.

This cautionary tale underscores the need for companies to strike a delicate balance between leveraging Big Data for innovation and considering the potential social impact. By ensuring ethical practices and respecting individual privacy, businesses can harness the power of data while fostering a positive relationship with their customers and society at large.

It is important to find the right balance between centralized control and local autonomy. On one hand, centralized control and coordination can help ensure consistency and alignment across different regions and business units. On the other hand, local autonomy and decision-making can enable organizations to respond quickly and effectively to local market conditions and customer needs.

It is essential to ensure that both the headquarters and the local business units are aligned and working toward the same goals. This can be achieved through clear communication, regular updates, and a strong governance framework that outlines the roles and responsibilities of different stakeholders.

Ultimately, finding the right balance can help organizations achieve the benefits of both centralized control and local autonomy, while avoiding potential conflicts and inefficiencies.

Speed of innovation

Are we innovating fast enough? is a common question. The pace of technological innovation and market disruption can be daunting, and businesses that fail to keep up risk being left behind. Here are some measures businesses can take to address this concern:

- **Adopt the law of urgency.** This emphasizes the importance of moving quickly and decisively, to capitalize on opportunities and stay ahead of the competition. This can involve creating a culture of innovation that encourages experimentation and risk-taking, as well as establishing processes and metrics to measure progress and success, all supported and challenged by deadlines.

- **Leverage technology such as AI and predictive analytics.** This will help identify emerging trends and opportunities. The use of agile methodologies such as DevOps can also help in rapidly developing and deploying new products and services.

- **Foster a mindset of continuous improvement and learning.** With this essential mindset, failures are viewed as opportunities to learn and grow, and feedback is used to refine and improve processes over time.

By taking these measures, businesses can position themselves to stay ahead of the innovation curve and thrive for the years to come.

Data breaches

Data analytics has become an increasingly essential aspect of business operations, but with this comes the need to ensure that the outcomes are accurate and reliable. There are several things that companies can do to be certain about data outcomes:

- **Establish a solid understanding of the data that is being used.** This means knowing where the data comes from, how it was collected, and how it has been processed. Without this knowledge, it is impossible to have confidence in the outcomes generated from the data.

- **Consider the quality of the data.** Poor-quality data can lead to inaccurate outcomes, which can have serious consequences for business decisions. To ensure data quality, companies should invest in data cleansing and validation processes, which help to identify and correct errors in the data, ensuring that it is accurate and reliable.

- **Review the methods used for data analysis.** Companies should have a clear understanding of the analytical techniques used and the assumptions made in the analysis. They should also have processes in place for verifying the results generated by these techniques. One way to verify the results is to use multiple analytical techniques. Companies can then compare the results generated by each technique and identify any inconsistencies or errors. This approach can also help to uncover new insights and patterns that may have been missed by using a single technique.

- **Assess the transparency of the data-analysis process.** Companies should have clear documentation of the data-analysis methods used, including the data sources, assumptions, and calculations made. This documentation should be made available to relevant stakeholders to ensure that everyone has a clear understanding of the data-analysis process.

- **Ensure the right people are involved in the data analytics process.** The team should have the necessary skills and expertise to conduct the analysis and interpret the results. Companies should also invest in training and development programs to ensure that their employees have the knowledge and skills needed to work with data effectively.

Despite taking these measures, companies still have concerns about the accuracy and reliability of data. The main concerns and mitigation measure are outlined in the table below.

Addressing concerns around data breaches

Concern	Further detail	Mitigation
Bias in the data analysis process	Bias can occur when there are preconceived notions or assumptions that influence the analysis or interpretation of the data	Use unbiased data-analysis methods and have a diverse team working on the analysis. This will help to ensure that different perspectives are considered and that there is no unconscious bias in the analysis process.
Data security	Lack of security around data, including protection from unauthorized access	Invest in data security measures such as encryption, access controls, and data backups.

Concern	Further detail	Mitigation
Data breaches	Potential for significant financial and reputational damage	Invest in data protection measures.
		Have a solid understanding of the data used, invest in data cleansing and validation processes, and use transparent data-analysis methods.
		Have the right people involved in the data analytics process and ensure that their data is secure and protected from unauthorized access.

By addressing these concerns, companies can have confidence in the outcomes generated from data analytics and make informed business decisions.

Social impact

Social impact is an increasingly important concern for businesses as customers, employees, and other stakeholders become more conscious of the social and environmental impact of business operations. To address this concern, companies must take the following steps to understand their social impact and develop strategies for reducing their negative impact and increasing their positive impact.

- **Conduct a social impact assessment.** This involves identifying the social and environmental effects of business operations and assessing the extent to which these effects are positive or negative. These assessments can help companies identify areas where they can improve their social impact and develop strategies to mitigate any negative effects.

- **Prioritize sustainability and Corporate Social Responsibility (CSR).** This means adopting sustainable business practices and taking responsibility for the social and environmental impact of business operations. It can include reducing carbon emissions, minimizing waste, and supporting local communities. To ensure that sustainability and CSR initiatives are effective, companies should set clear goals and targets and regularly monitor their progress. They should also engage with stakeholders— including customers, employees, and local communities—to understand their concerns and priorities, and to build support for sustainability and CSR initiatives.

- **Consider the social impact of their data analytics initiatives.** This includes ensuring that data is collected and used in a way that respects privacy and is ethical. Companies should also be transparent about how data is collected and used, and give customers control over their own data.

By taking these steps, companies can reduce their negative impact and increase their positive impact, and build a stronger relationship with customers, employees, and other stakeholders.

Typical concerns of CIOs

In today's rapidly evolving technological landscape, chief information officers (CIOs) face a multitude of critical concerns that demand their constant attention and strategic decision-making. As the senior executives responsible for overseeing an organization's information technology and digital infrastructure, CIOs grapple with challenges ranging from cybersecurity threats and data breaches, to managing complex IT projects, thereby ensuring seamless digital transformation and aligning technology initiatives with broader business goals. Balancing innovation with risk management, CIOs play a pivotal role in shaping the technological future of their organizations and navigating the ever-changing demands of the digital era.

The concerns and challenges faced by CIOs are shown in the table below.

Main concerns for CIOs

Concern	Further detail	Mitigation
Resistance to change	Some stakeholders are hesitant to embrace new technologies or ways of working, and efforts to implement digital transformation initiatives.	Communicate the benefits of digital transformation clearly and demonstrate how it will improve operations, efficiency, and productivity. Engage stakeholders in the planning process and involve them in decision-making, to build buy-in and ensure stakeholders' concerns are heard and addressed.
Legacy systems	Older systems and technology may be deeply ingrained within an organization, making it difficult to upgrade or implement new solutions without significant disruption.	Upgrading/replacing legacy systems can be daunting task, but it's important to prioritize this work to avoid falling behind competitors. A phased approach can help, focusing on smaller systems or processes first to build momentum and demonstrate success. Collaboration with other departments and stakeholders can help ensure that the new systems meet the needs of the business.

Concern	Further detail	Mitigation
Lack of IT talent	Finding and retaining skilled IT professionals can be challenging, particularly in highly competitive industries or in regions with a shortage of tech talent.	Consider partnering with educational institutions to develop a pipeline of talent. Investing in employee training and development can also help build internal expertise. Leveraging external contractors or consultants can provide additional resources when needed.
Budget constraints	Projects can be expensive, and securing funding for them can be a challenge, especially if they are not seen as directly contributing to the bottom line.	Create a well-crafted business case, with clear financial projections. Partner with other departments or organizations to share costs and maximize resources. Negotiate with finance to create a profit center, to function like a research and development fund. This allows the company to allocate funds for big investments, without having to account for every penny; and ensures the cost of the project is equally distributed across the organization, not shouldered by the first movers.

Here are some further steps to help ensure that digital transformation initiatives receive the attention necessary to succeed.

- **Identifying systems and processes that will be affected by the new solution:** This is the first step toward meeting funding requirements. Work with suppliers or internal IT teams to develop a plan for integration. Pilot testing can help identify any issues early on and ensure that the new system is functioning as expected.

- **Cybersecurity risks:** Ensuring that adequate cybersecurity measures are in place is a top priority for CIOs. Protecting against cyber threats requires a multifaceted approach, combining technology, timely software updates, policies, and training. Ensure that all systems and data are protected by up-to-date antivirus and malware software, and implement strict access controls and user-authentication processes.

- **Regular training and awareness programs:** These can help educate employees on best practices for data protection and cyber hygiene.

- **Interoperability:** Integrating new systems and technologies with existing infrastructure can be complex and may require extensive testing and customization to ensure interoperability. Careful planning and testing are vital to ensuring that new systems and technologies can be integrated with existing infrastructure.

- **Lack of alignment:** To be effective, digital transformation initiatives must align with the overall business strategy and goals. However, achieving this alignment can be a challenge, particularly in large and complex organizations with multiple departments and stakeholders. To ensure that digital transformation initiatives align with business goals, it's important to involve stakeholders from across the organization in the planning process. Regular communication and collaboration can help ensure that everyone is working toward the same objectives. Consider establishing a governance structure, or steering committee, to oversee the initiative and provide guidance on priorities and resource allocation. Trusted employees can regularly check the effectiveness of the steering committee.

Summary

While the benefits of carefully planned and executed digital transformation far outweigh the challenges involved, it is inevitable that you will need to over-come some resistance and concerns. This chapter has outlined the main concerns and ways to address them:

- Companies may fear that implementing digital transformation initiatives will result in a loss of control. Agile DevOps methodologies prioritize flexibility and collaboration while maintaining centralized control.

- Companies can prioritize innovation as a core value, while being mindful of the risks and challenges that come with it, such as data breaches and bias in the data-analysis process.

- Companies must prioritize transparency and accountability in their data practices and be mindful of the potential misuse of Big Data.

- To align digital transformation initiatives with business goals, CIOs can:

  - Involve stakeholders in the planning process

  - Prioritize upgrading legacy systems

  - Partner with educational institutions

  - Create a business case for investment

  - Implement cybersecurity measures

  - Carefully plan and test integration of new systems

  - Involve stakeholders in the planning process

  - Establish a governance structure or steering committee to oversee the initiative

  - Ensure regular communication and collaboration about the project and the benefits of digital transformation

10
Looking Further Ahead— The Big Picture

It's important to have a clear understanding of where you are and where you want to go in your digital transformation. To achieve this, it's crucial to be able to walk the gemba (visit the center of operations) and see for yourself what's happening on the ground.

This isn't only about the immediate future. To succeed in the long term, you need to be able to think further ahead and connect the dots to see the bigger picture. This means having a clear vision of where you want to be, and having the ability to identify the risks and opportunities that lie ahead.

Linking perspectives—bringing together different viewpoints and skill sets in your team—allows you to benefit from that range of expertise.

Walking the gemba

Seeing things for yourself—walking the gemba—is a crucial first step in driving success within any organization. This approach involves physically or virtually going to where the work is done and observing the processes and interactions firsthand. Letting others come to your boardroom desk doesn't reveal the real issues—the reality is filtered before it reaches you.

By walking the gemba, leaders can:

- Gain a deeper understanding of the current state of operations

- Identify potential inefficiencies or areas for improvement

- Develop a plan for immediate next steps

Immediate next steps are the actions required to address the issues or opportunities identified during the gemba walk. They can range from small adjustments to processes or policies, to more significant personnel or technology changes. The key is to be proactive and act quickly, to avoid potential negative consequences.

While identifying and addressing immediate next steps is essential during the gemba walk, it's also important to keep an eye on the future. This means having a clear vision of where the organization wants to be in the long term and identifying the trends, opportunities, and challenges that may arise. By seeing the future, leaders can develop a plan for the strategic initiatives and investments needed to achieve their goals.

Connecting the dots is another crucial aspect of walking the gemba. This involves taking a holistic approach to identify the interconnections between different parts of the organization and how they contribute to the overall success. When leaders visit different departments and encourage discussions among different teams, feedback is shared and collaboration improves. Opening up communication channels in this way can lead to unexpected solutions and improved work processes. Leaders need to be able to see beyond the silos and individual departments to understand how they fit into the bigger picture. They also need to identify opportunities for collaboration and integration, leading to increased efficiency and better results.

Learning from the risks identified during the gemba walk, it is key to add these to a new or renewed risk model as an essential tool for leaders to identify and manage potential risks to the organization's success. This involves assessing the likelihood and impact of different scenarios such as changes in the market, regulations, or technology. By developing a risk model, leaders can make informed decisions about resource allocation and mitigate potential negative outcomes.

Walking the gemba is a crucial first step in driving success within an organization and if you have applied the metaverse in your company, this means you don't even have to go too far to do it.

Tomorrow begins today

In our rapidly changing world, the future is no longer a distant horizon but a reality that is unfolding before our very eyes. With so many challenges and opportunities on the horizon, there is no time to waste. That's why it's crucial to start acting today. By researching, analyzing, planning, and innovating, you can pave the way for a better tomorrow.

Of course, you can't do it all alone. Collaboration is key. You might need to partner with peers, seek out the expertise of your competitors, or tap into the knowledge of your colleagues to achieve your goals. By working together, you can leverage your collective strengths and overcome your weaknesses.

However, innovation also requires individual effort. You need to be willing to take risks, experiment with new ideas, and challenge the status quo. That means fostering a mindset of creativity and innovation. One way to do this is by thinking outside the box and exploring unconventional solutions. It also means deliberately disrupting your own system to spark new ideas and drive paradigm shifts.

Don't wait for the future to arrive—start building it today. By acting, collaborating with others, and fostering your own creativity and innovation, you can create a better tomorrow for yourself and for the world.

At the start of my career, we had recently implemented a system for client securities. However, shortly after the implementation, we encountered an issue in settlement and had to undo 21,000 transactions. Unfortunately, the system didn't have the necessary functionality to handle this, and we were in deep trouble.

As a system administrator at the time, I had just seen a demo of a test tool that could automate user actions by recording them and replaying them as a test user. I realized that this tool could be repurposed for our problem by teaching it how to navigate the undo screen used by our coworkers. Despite the risks, I managed to persuade my senior management to let me use the test tool in production. This solution became the prototype for screen-scraping tools, which became popular in the early 2000s. This is how creativity and innovation can arise from collaboration and learning, in response to needs that arise within an organization.

Linking perspectives

Linking company perspectives is a powerful way to drive innovation, increase efficiency, and ultimately achieve sustained success. You can start by viewing your company as a triangle of three entities: people, processes, and technology. By bringing together diverse perspectives from these areas—including of course the business perspective—you can gain a holistic understanding of your organization and identify areas for improvement.

For example, by understanding how technology fits into the overall process and how people interact with it, leaders can develop targeted training programs that ensure efficient migration to new processes. Linking perspectives in this way identifies opportunities to train employees in new technologies.

Another way to view the triangle is to set up confidants at every level of the organization. These trusted advisers help leaders to verify their own observations and ensure leaders are not sitting in an ivory tower, unaware of others' perspectives. This approach fosters a culture of collaboration and ensures that all voices are heard.

Benefits of linking perspectives include improved decision-making, increased efficiency, and a better understanding of the organization's strengths and weaknesses. By bringing together different viewpoints and expertise, leaders can identify opportunities for innovation and growth as well as potential threats. This approach fosters a culture of continuous improvement and ensures the organization is always moving forward.

The mountain of value within

To succeed in today's fast-paced business environment, organizations must be able to tap into the talents and skills of their people. Talent is a crucial component of success, and it sits within your organization. By connecting with your people and investing in their development, you can unlock their potential and drive innovation. However, many organizations struggle to find the value within their workforce and therefore miss out on opportunities for growth and innovation.

Connecting with your people and uncovering the mountain of value within requires a shift in mindset. Leaders must be willing to listen to their employees and give them the support they need to succeed. This may involve, for example, investing in training and development programs, or creating opportunities for cross-functional collaboration. Whatever the approach, the key is to create an environment where employees feel valued and supported, and where their talents are recognized and rewarded.

The power of engagement

The power of engagement cannot be overstated. When people are engaged, they are more productive, more creative, and more likely to be satisfied with their work. Engagement is not just an individual attribute, however—it is contagious. When one person is engaged, it inspires others to follow suit. This is so important; engagement spreads like wildfire throughout an organization.

Engagement is not just a passive state—it can be actively cultivated and nurtured. In fact, the most successful organizations are those that create a culture of engagement—one that values collaboration, communication, and empowerment. When people feel like they are part of something bigger than themselves, and when they feel their work matters and that they are making a difference, they are more likely to be engaged.

In 2007–2012 I was part of a program to merge two banks into one. This was a massive undertaking, which required a great deal of coordination and hard work. One day a manager gathered us together and spoke about the privilege we had to be working on such a unique and important program. "This is a once-in-a-lifetime experience," he said. "You have been chosen for the tasks ahead of you, and your work will make a real difference." I remember feeling a surge of excitement and purpose at his words. Even simple gestures of recognition can have an enormous impact on engagement, and his words motivated me to work even harder to ensure the success of the program.

When engagement is widespread, it can become a movement. By rallying people around a common purpose, by inspiring them to act, and by creating a sense of shared ownership and responsibility, you can start a movement that drives real change. Whether you are leading a team, managing a project, or simply trying to make a difference in your own life, remember the power of engagement. It can be the catalyst that propels you to success.

Uncovering hidden value

By engaging with employees and understanding their unique talents, leaders can identify where those employees contribute the most value. This approach fosters a culture of collaboration and empowers employees to take ownership of their work, leading to increased job satisfaction and higher levels of engagement.

Another key aspect of finding the mountain of value within is recognizing that talent sits within every level of the organization. From entry-level positions to C-suite executives, each employee has their own unique set of skills and experiences that can contribute to the success of the organization. By taking the time to identify and develop these talents, leaders can tap into a wealth of knowledge and expertise that might otherwise go unnoticed and unused. By creating a safe environment, giving permission to excel, nurturing a community vibe, and encouraging people to explore their talents, organizations can achieve higher levels of success and foster a culture of continuous improvement. Take the time to invest in your people and uncover the hidden value within your organization—the results may surprise you.

Return on investment

Management development programs have traditionally been aimed at a target group, from recent graduates to those in their forties. Those selected for the programs received recognition in the first half of their career and therefore feel capable of making a difference. Unfortunately, after companies have developed this group, they tend to focus on new talents. Their former rising stars become a forgotten cohort who, due to their developed mindset, have a great chance of making the money invested in them profitable elsewhere in society.

This pool of established talent represents a wealth of expertise, which can be activated with simple measures such as extending the feedback loop, mentoring new talent by former talent, and job rotation between former talent. This can lead to increased job satisfaction and an even greater return on investment. Especially while there is scarcity of qualified personnel, it is certainly worth considering these measures.

The role of citizen development

Citizen development has emerged as a transformative force within organizations, revolutionizing the way applications and solutions are developed. By empowering non-technical employees to create custom solutions using low-code or no-code platforms, citizen development enables organizations to accelerate their digital transformation journey and drive innovation.

Here are just some of the advantages that can be realized:

- **Time efficiency.** Traditional application development processes can be time-consuming, requiring extensive planning and coordination between business units and IT departments. By contrast, citizen development enables employees to create their own applications quickly, bypassing traditional development processes and the associated bureaucracy. This enables organizations to rapidly prototype new solutions, test them, and iterate until they find the right fit for their needs.

- **Cost efficiency.** Traditional application development is expensive, requiring specialized technical skills and IT infrastructure. This can create a significant bottleneck, limiting the pace of innovation and creating frustration for employees who need new solutions. Citizen development, on the other hand, requires little to no specialized technical expertise, and can be completed using low-code or no-code platforms, especially cloud solutions based on pay per use. Faster and cheaper solutions make this a compelling proposition for organizations looking to optimize their resources.

- **Creativity.** Citizen development has the potential to foster a culture of innovation and problem-solving within organizations. By empowering employees to take ownership of the tools they use in their work, organizations can unleash a wealth of creativity and ingenuity that might otherwise go untapped. For example, a salesperson might use a low-code platform to create a customized app that helps them manage their leads and sales progress more effectively. This means they not only solve a problem for themselves but also create a valuable solution that can be shared across the organization. Similarly, a customer service representative might use a no-code platform to automate routine tasks, freeing up time to focus on more complex and value-adding activities.

- **Collaboration.** Citizen development offers an opportunity to bridge the gap between business units and IT departments. Traditionally, these two groups have operated in silos, with the IT department often viewed as a bottleneck to innovation. Citizen development can help to break down these silos by enabling business units to take a more active role in developing the tools they need to do their jobs effectively. This can create a sense of shared ownership and responsibility, fostering a more collaborative and productive relationship between business units and IT departments.

To be successful, citizen development initiatives require careful planning and management. Organizations need to establish guidelines and standards around the use of low-code and no-code platforms, to ensure that applications are developed in a way that is secure, scalable, and aligned with the organization's overall strategy. They must also take governing bodies' concerns on risk and financial management into account and be sure to enforce legislation in these areas. In addition, organizations need to provide training and support to employees to ensure that they have the skills and knowledge required to develop applications effectively.

In conclusion, citizen development has the potential to transform the way organizations develop applications and solutions. By empowering non-technical employees to become innovators and problem solvers, citizen development can accelerate digital transformation, drive innovation, and foster a culture of collaboration and problem-solving. With careful planning and management, organizations can harness the power of citizen development to drive their business forward and stay ahead of the competition.

Exploring metaverse solutions

Although hybrid working and tools like Zoom and Microsoft Teams means remote contact possibilities have improved, there is currently no substitute for sitting at a desk next to colleagues. At the time of writing, the metaverse is evolving fast, making it something worth focusing on for the future.

The first companies are already enriching their company engagement via onboarding to the metaverse, in combination with their own office software. The extra costs are minor compared with office tools, and by reducing travel costs, metaverse solutions will even incur significant cost savings and reduce the environmental footprint.

Quarterly central board meetings could be replaced by twice-yearly meetings in the metaverse—exactly the same meetings as those you might currently be holding in a conference room at a hotel. If you're at a metaverse conference, you can still go to a central hall during a break, watch a promo video of your company, and have a virtual coffee with a colleague to discuss it. You can visit a colleague abroad in the metaverse, even attending a board meeting of that colleague and whiteboarding some ideas together, as if you were present at the same place.

If you onboard your whole company, you can virtually visit your factory assembly lines (see the section on walking the gemba, earlier). You can reduce your environmental footprint and save huge amounts in travel expenses, and still achieve the same impact.

Is hybrid working causing your employees to feel less sense of community? In the metaverse you could set office times, where the whole team needs to be present for set hours of the day. This provides the benefits of working physically together and of the engagement that brings.

You could bring some of your business into the most visited metaverse. You could even sell your goods in a virtual world, where they can be ordered and transferred to the customer in his real home, wherever he resides on our planet.

The endless possibilities that come with metaverse development make it an area no successful organization can ignore.

Assessing the organization's fitness for change

Assessing the health of an organization is a critical step in the change management process. It allows leaders to identify areas of weakness and to implement strategies for improvement. However, assessing fitness for change is not a simple task. It requires a multifaceted approach that considers factors including:

- **Advanced analytics.** This can play a crucial role in assessing organizational fitness for change. By collecting and analyzing data on employee engagement, productivity, and other key metrics, leaders can identify areas of the organization that require attention and improvement.

The data can also be used to track progress over time and measure the effectiveness of change management initiatives.

- **Innovation labs.** These labs provide a physical space for employees to experiment with new ideas and technologies, and they can be used to test and refine change management strategies. It is important to ensure that these labs are integrated into the broader organizational culture, and that their findings are communicated effectively throughout the organization.

- **Culture and mentality.** Leaders must be aware of the existing culture and mindset within the organization and take steps to address any barriers to change. This may involve implementing training and development programs to promote a culture of innovation, or creating incentives for employees to embrace change.

Assessing organizational change fitness requires a holistic approach that considers all these factors. By using advanced analytics to collect data, introducing innovation labs to test new ideas, and promoting a culture of innovation and change, organizations can become as change-ready as possible.

It is important to remember that change is a continuous process, and that ongoing monitoring and evaluation are essential to ensure that the organization remains healthy and adaptable to an ever-changing business environment.

Assessing the organization's operational health

Operational health refers to the effectiveness and efficiency of the organization's day-to-day operations, which is essential for achieving long-term success.

To assess operational health, organizations must first identify their KPIs such as customer satisfaction, product quality, and employee productivity. By collecting and analyzing data on these KPIs, leaders can identify areas of the organization that require attention and implement strategies for improvement.

One way to improve operational health is by adopting Lean principles, which focus on eliminating waste and maximizing value for customers.[28] This may involve streamlining processes, improving supply chain management, or implementing new technologies to automate repetitive tasks.

Another key factor in operational health is employee engagement. Engaged employees are more productive, better for the consumer experience, and more

---

28   D Do, "The five principles of Lean", The Lean Way blog (August 5 2017), https://theleanway.net/The-Five-Principles-of-Lean, accessed September 19, 2023

likely to stay long term with the organization, which can have a positive impact on the bottom line. To improve employee engagement, organizations may need to implement training and development programs, create a positive work environment, or provide opportunities for career advancement.

Ultimately, assessing and improving operational health is about creating a culture of continuous improvement that allows the organization to adapt to changing business conditions and stay ahead of the competition. By adopting a data-driven approach to operations management, organizations can identify areas of weakness and implement strategies for improvement, resulting in increased efficiency, higher productivity, and greater customer satisfaction.

Summary

By leveraging the benefits of your triangle (people, processes, and technology), you can achieve sustained success and thrive in a constantly evolving business landscape. Other techniques for improving your current and future position include:

- Walking the gemba and connecting the dots so you can improve your current policies and process as well as planning for the future

- Taking a holistic approach to identify the interconnections between different parts of the organization and how they contribute to the overall success

- Bringing together different viewpoints and skill sets so you can benefit from the diverse expertise of your team and link perspectives

- Explore the transformative and innovative power citizen development can bring to your organization

- Getting the most from your talent by unlocking your people's potential, including emphasis on:

  - Powerful engagement with your teams

  - Employees' hidden values

  - Focus on employees you have invested in

  - The possibilities of citizen development

- Exploring the fast-developing world of metaverse business opportunities

- Assessing organizational fitness for change, with a multifaceted approach, to stay ahead of the curve

- Assessing operational health and improving the effectiveness and efficiency of the organization's day-to-day operations to achieve long-term success

Conclusion

Throughout these pages, we have explored the theme of innovation from within and how it can be harnessed to drive progress and success in our personal and professional lives. As I conclude, I want to leave you with some final reflections on the key themes we have covered.

Innovation from within is not just a concept. It is a mindset that drives success in today's fast-paced and ever-changing world. By recognizing and leveraging the talents within your organization and within yourself, you can unleash a wave of creativity that can lead to breakthroughs in product development, customer engagement, and overall business success.

Embracing this mindset requires a willingness to challenge the status quo and to take risks. With the right tools and support, you can create a culture of innovation that inspires everyone to think differently, act boldly, and drive meaningful change. It is only by cultivating a mindset of creativity, curiosity, and collaboration that we can truly unlock our full potential.

I'm fortunate to have found a great partner to entrepreneur with as well as a supportive employer who encourages side activities. These side activities have helped me broaden my horizons, gain inspiration, and ultimately bring more value to the company where I work. This "prosperity loop" concept is incredibly important in today's business world. By encouraging individuals to pursue their passions outside of work, we can create a more motivated, creative, and engaged workforce.

I hope this book has inspired you to embrace the power of innovation from within and to act toward creating a better future, both for yourself and for those around you, using all my tips, including my RAPID Digital Transformation Model.

You can hire me to assess and monitor your change portfolio, as a holistic coach and mentor, or (as cofounder of AnswerInside Metaverse Solutions) as an adviser on augmented/virtual reality. I invite you to visit my landing page, where you can find more information about my work and the topics discussed in this book. Join my mailing list to stay up to date, and let's work together to achieve your vision.

Further reading

Here is a list of other useful works that I recommend.

Bos, J et al., *Project-Driven Creation* (Phaos, 2014)

Coppenhagen, R, *Creatieregie Visie en verbinding bij verandering* (Scriptum, 2006)

Gene, K et al., *The Phoenix Project: A Novel About IT, DevOps, and Helping Your Business Win* (It Revolution Press, 2013)

Hoogveld, M, *Agile managen: Snel en wendbaar werken aan continue verbetering in organisaties* (Van Duuren Management, 2017)

Mouchtak, M, *The Sustainable Turnaround: Fix, Reset and Accelerate Your Business to Thrive in 12 Months* (Rethink Press, 2021)

Parker, GG et al., *Platform Revolution: How Networked Markets Are Transforming the Economy and How to Make Them Work for You* (WW Norton & Co, 2016)

Sanders T, *Love Is the Killer App: How to Win Business and Influence Friends* (Crown Publishing Group, 2002)

Acknowledgments

I want to give a big thank-you to some amazing people who played a crucial role in making this book happen. They offered their help and ideas, and it really made a difference.

Foremost, I extend my heartfelt appreciation to my beta readers: Johan Zwart, Buco Taschner, Michiel van Vliet, John Heideman, and Harry Oosterhuis. Their commitment to reviewing early versions of the book and providing invaluable feedback has been instrumental in shaping its evolution. Their guidance and insights have been pivotal, and I am truly indebted to them for sharing their time and expertise.

I wish to express my deepest thanks to Amir Arooni, whose generosity in immediately offering his time and penning the foreword has touched me deeply.

My gratitude also extends to my friends and colleagues, whose unyielding encouragement and belief in me have empowered me to share my ideas and aspirations with the world.

Throughout my journey, I have been fortunate to draw inspiration from the following remarkable individuals who have left an indelible impact on their respective fields.

Bart Veugelers showed me the importance of being determined and disciplined. He always worked hard to achieve his goals and never gave up, which really impressed me. His friendship during tough times was also a bright spot for me.

Frank Molling taught me about being honest and good at understanding complicated things. He was great at taking a lot of information and making it easy to understand, so important decisions could be made.

Harry Oosterhuis, my teaching partner, was a great leader and showed me how to lead by example and help others learn.

Guido Schilder was like my partner in crime during tough situations. We helped each other out when things got tricky.

Johan Zwart was the ultimate problem-solver. He was able to fix all sorts of issues, and he did it by showing a lot of trust.

This book is also a big shout-out to many others who might not be named here but who still made a big impact. To everyone who gave me advice, shared their thoughts, and supported me along the way, I am truly grateful.

Lastly, I want to thank God for His wisdom and everlasting inspiration. His grace and blessings have sustained me through the highs and lows of life, and I am forever grateful for His presence in my life.

In the end, this book is all about the power of working together, learning from each other, and finding inspiration. All the people I've mentioned here, and many others, helped make this book possible. As we read through the pages, let's keep the spirit of teamwork and shared knowledge in mind. These lessons can help us make positive changes in the world of digital leadership.

The Author

Tjeerd has more than thirty years' experience in leading local and global IT (platform) transformations. As the global IT platform transformation lead at ING, Tjeerd has successfully led numerous projects that have revolutionized the banking industry, most recently the transformation of the technology platform foundation. He is a master of innovation and transformation management who has been at the forefront of digitization, always having a keen understanding of advanced technologies such as AR/VR. He is a cofounder of AnswerInside Metaverse Solutions, which advises businesses on onboarding to the metaverse and creating virtual company environments in AR/VR.

Tjeerd is a highly skilled business coach, who has assisted companies and executives in achieving their goals. His client list includes prominent names such as PwC, ING, and various Dutch government bodies. His approach is both holistic and personalized, as he takes into account the distinct needs and challenges of each individual.

Tjeerd's ability to identify and implement emerging technologies has helped organizations stay ahead of the curve and drive growth. He has been a trusted adviser to some of the world's most respected company leaders.

Tjeerd's credibility is well established in the industry. He has been invited to speak at numerous occasions, sharing his insights on innovation, digital transformation, and business coaching. His presentations are always insightful, engaging, and practical, leaving audiences with actionable takeaways. He is passionate about sharing his knowledge and helping others succeed.

Tjeerd studied at the Inholland University of Applied Sciences and followed this with a postgraduate qualification in life coaching at Atma Academy.

🌐 www.innovationfromwithin.eu

in www.linkedin.com/in/tjeerd-hunnekens-307a893